1st Edition
Ferros Publishing © 2024
Author: Maxwell Sterling
ISBN: 9798882637742

Disclaimer

This book is intended for informational and educational purposes only. The content provided within these pages is a general overview of Artificial Intelligence (AI) and its applications and should not be taken as professional advice or instruction. While the authors and publishers have made every effort to ensure the accuracy and completeness of the information contained in this book, the rapidly evolving nature of AI technology means that some specifics may change over time. Therefore, we cannot guarantee that all information presented will remain accurate at the time of the reader's engagement with this material.

The authors and publishers disclaim any liability for any direct, indirect, incidental, or consequential damages or losses that may result from the use of the information in this book. This includes, but is not limited to, errors or omissions in the content, any actions taken based on the information provided, and the outcomes of using the techniques and recommendations detailed herein.

Readers are encouraged to conduct their own research and consult with professionals in the field of AI before applying any of the concepts, strategies, or technologies discussed in this book to personal or professional projects. The examples and case studies provided are for illustrative purposes only and do not imply endorsement of specific technologies or platforms.

By proceeding beyond this disclaimer, readers acknowledge and accept the limitations of the information provided and agree to hold harmless the authors, publishers, and any affiliated parties from any claims or actions related to the use or application of the content found within this book.

INTRODUCTION

In the heart of the digital age, a revolution quietly unfolds, reshaping the fabric of our society, economy, and personal lives. This revolution is not led by armies or governed by political movements; it is propelled forward by an invisible force that has integrated into our daily existence almost without notice. Artificial Intelligence (AI) – a term that once conjured images of science fiction and distant futures – has become a tangible, driving force of the present, transforming industries, enhancing human capabilities, and challenging our understanding of what it means to be intelligent.

This book is a journey into the essence of AI, designed to demystify the complexities and illuminate the practicalities of engaging with this technology. Whether you are a student, professional, enthusiast, or simply a curious mind, the pages that follow are crafted to provide a comprehensive overview of AI's foundational principles, its myriad applications, and the profound impact it holds for our collective future.

We stand at the precipice of a new era, where AI's potential to augment human intelligence presents unprecedented opportunities for innovation, creativity, and problem-solving. Yet, with great power comes great responsibility. The ethical considerations, societal impacts, and philosophical questions surrounding AI demand thoughtful exploration and dialogue. This book aims to foster such discussions, encouraging readers to contemplate not only the technical aspects of AI but also the broader implications of its integration into our world.

Through a blend of expert insights, real-world examples, and practical advice, we will navigate the landscapes of machine learning, deep learning, robotics, and more. We will uncover the mechanisms that enable machines to learn from data, make decisions, and perform tasks that were once the exclusive domain of humans. Beyond the technology itself, we will examine the role of AI in addressing some of the most pressing challenges of our time, from climate change to healthcare, and explore the pathways it opens for innovation across various sectors.

As we embark on this exploration, our goal is not only to inform but also to inspire. AI is not a distant reality to be passively observed; it is a dynamic field where each of us can play a role in shaping its evolution and harnessing its potential for the betterment of humanity. Whether you aim to contribute to AI research, implement AI solutions in your industry, or simply understand the changes unfolding around you, this book is your gateway to the fascinating world of Artificial Intelligence.

TABLE OF CONTENTS

CHAPTER 1: INTRODUCTION TO ARTIFICIAL INTELLIGENCE

CONCEPT OF ARTIFICIAL INTELLIGENCE

Imagine you're walking through a bustling city street, effortlessly navigating through crowds, recognizing faces of friends in an instant, and making countless decisions, like when to cross the road or duck to avoid a low-hanging branch. This incredible ability to perceive, understand, and interact with the world comes so naturally to us humans that we rarely stop to think about how complex these tasks actually are. This innate capability is a product of human intelligence, a blend of learning, reasoning, and self-correction that has been honed over millennia.

Now, enter the realm of Artificial Intelligence (AI), a field of computer science dedicated to creating machines that can mimic these human-like abilities. But how does AI manage to do this, and how does it differ from the natural intelligence we, and other living beings, possess?

At its core, AI is about programming computers to make decisions, learn from data, and perform tasks that would typically require human intelligence. This includes everything from understanding spoken words (like Siri or Alexa responding to your questions), recognizing faces in photos (think of how Facebook tags friends in pictures), to beating world champions in complex games like chess or Go.

The key difference between AI and human intelligence lies in how learning and decision-making happen. Human intelligence is deeply rooted in biological processes, involving emotions, consciousness, and a highly flexible form of learning that's influenced by our environment, culture, and personal experiences. We learn from our mistakes, adapt to new situations, and can understand context in a nuanced way that AI currently cannot match.

AI, on the other hand, learns from vast amounts of data. It identifies patterns, makes predictions, or takes actions based on the programming and algorithms created by humans. For example, an AI designed to recognize dogs in photographs has likely been trained on thousands (or even millions) of images, learning to identify features that define what a dog looks like. However, if you show it something slightly out of the ordinary—say, a dog wearing a costume— it might struggle to recognize it as a dog because it hasn't been explicitly trained on that type of data.

This learning process is what sets apart different types of AI. Narrow AI, or Weak AI, is programmed to perform a specific task (like the dog recognition example) and doesn't possess understanding or consciousness. It's what most AI technologies are today: highly specialized tools that excel in particular domains but can't generalize their intelligence to a wide range of tasks like a human can.

General AI, or Strong AI, which remains a theoretical concept for now, would be capable of understanding, learning, and applying its intelligence broadly, just like a human. It would not only recognize a dog in any costume but could also understand the concept of "costume" and apply that knowledge in completely different contexts, something that's second nature to humans but a monumental challenge for AI developers.

In summary, while AI can perform tasks that seem intelligent and sometimes even surpass human abilities in specific domains, it operates fundamentally differently from human or natural intelligence. AI's "thought processes" are confined to the parameters set by its programming and the data it's been trained on, lacking the emotional depth, consciousness, and generalization capabilities that come naturally to living beings. As we continue to advance in the field of AI, bridging this gap remains one of the most fascinating and challenging frontiers.

CORE OBJECTIVES OF AI

Diving into the world of Artificial Intelligence (AI) is like exploring a vast ocean of possibilities where machines are not just tools but partners in our quest to understand and interact with the world around us. At the heart of AI lie several core objectives that serve as the guiding stars for this exploration. These objectives—reasoning, knowledge representation, planning, learning, natural language processing (NLP), perception, and the ability to move and manipulate objects—outline the capabilities we aspire to instil in machines. Let's navigate through these objectives in an informative yet friendly manner.

REASONING: THE POWER OF LOGIC AND DECISION-MAKING

Imagine you're trying to solve a puzzle. You look at the pieces, think about where they might fit, and through a process of trial and error, you start to see the bigger picture. This is reasoning—the ability to solve problems through logical deduction and inference. In AI, reasoning enables machines to solve complex problems, from diagnosing diseases based on symptoms to proving mathematical theorems. It's about giving machines the ability to think logically and make decisions based on the information they have.

KNOWLEDGE REPRESENTATION: THE ART OF STORING AND USING INFORMATION

Knowledge representation is akin to creating a map of information that AI systems can use to navigate the world. It involves encoding information about the world in a format that a computer can understand and process. This could be anything from the rules of a language to the layout of a city or the relationships between different concepts. By representing knowledge in a structured way, AI systems can perform tasks like answering questions, making recommendations, or even composing music.

PLANNING: CHARTING THE COURSE TO ACHIEVE GOALS

Planning in AI is about figuring out the steps needed to achieve a specific goal, much like planning a trip. It involves considering various actions, predicting their outcomes, and then selecting the best sequence of actions to reach the desired end state. This capability is crucial in robotics, autonomous vehicles, and managing complex logistics, where machines must navigate through physical or computational environments to accomplish tasks efficiently and effectively.

LEARNING: THE JOURNEY OF GROWTH AND ADAPTATION

Learning is the cornerstone of human development, and it's no different in AI. Machine learning, a subset of AI, focuses on giving machines the ability to learn from data, improve over time, and make predictions or decisions without being explicitly programmed for every possible scenario. This is how recommendation systems learn your preferences, how voice assistants get better at understanding you, and how autonomous cars adapt to new driving conditions.

NATURAL LANGUAGE PROCESSING (NLP): UNDERSTANDING AND GENERATING HUMAN LANGUAGE

NLP is the magic that allows machines to understand and generate human language. It's what powers chatbots, translation services, and voice-activated assistants. Through NLP, AI systems can interpret text and speech, grasp the nuances of language, and even detect sentiment or generate text that sounds convincingly human. It's about bridging the gap between human communication and machine understanding.

PERCEPTION: SEEING AND INTERPRETING THE WORLD

Perception in AI is about enabling machines to interpret and understand sensory information from the world around them. This could be visual information captured by cameras, sound waves picked up by microphones, or even data from sensors that detect temperature or pressure. AI systems with perception capabilities can recognize faces, interpret gestures, navigate environments, and interact with the physical world in ways that were once the realm of science fiction.

MOVEMENT AND MANIPULATION: INTERACTING WITH THE PHYSICAL WORLD

Finally, the ability to move and manipulate objects is what brings AI into the physical realm. This is the domain of robotics, where AI systems control physical machines that can move, grasp, and manipulate objects. From robotic arms assembling cars on a production line to drones delivering packages, this aspect of AI combines software and hardware to perform tasks that require physical interaction with the world.

Together, these objectives form the foundation of AI's quest to create machines that can think, learn, and interact with the world in ways that mimic human intelligence. Each objective represents a piece of the puzzle, and as we advance in these areas, we move closer to realizing the full potential of AI in enhancing our lives and reshaping our future.

CONCEPT OF COGNITIVE COMPUTING

Embark on a journey into the fascinating world of cognitive computing, a realm where machines are not just calculators or data processors, but entities that can mimic the intricate tapestry of human thought. Cognitive computing represents the frontier of artificial intelligence (AI), where the goal is not merely to create systems that can perform tasks, but to forge ones that can understand, reason, learn, and interact in a way that is remarkably human-like.

THE ESSENCE OF COGNITIVE COMPUTING

Imagine for a moment the complexity of human cognition. Our brains process vast amounts of information from our senses, analyze it, make decisions, learn from experiences, and interact with our environment—all in real-time and often without conscious effort. Cognitive computing seeks to emulate this incredible capacity within a computerized model, creating systems that can analyze data, grasp its meaning, and make decisions or generate responses that require a form of understanding.

SIMULATING HUMAN THOUGHT PROCESSES

At the heart of cognitive computing is the ambition to simulate human thought processes in a nuanced and sophisticated manner. This involves several key components:

Understanding Natural Language: Just as humans communicate through complex languages, cognitive computing systems are designed to understand and interpret human language in all its subtleties, allowing for more natural and intuitive interactions between humans and machines.

Learning and Reasoning: Like a curious child exploring the world, cognitive systems learn from the data they are exposed to, using it to reason and make decisions. This learning isn't just about memorizing facts but involves understanding concepts, patterns, and even the context within which information is presented.

Sensory Processing: Cognitive computing also extends to the ability to process and interpret sensory data—seeing, hearing, and touching—much like humans do. This allows these systems to analyze images, understand spoken words, and interact with the physical world in a more human-like manner.

Emotional Intelligence: Beyond just processing information, cognitive systems aim to recognize and even simulate emotions. By understanding the emotional context of interactions, these systems can provide responses that are more empathetic and appropriate, enhancing the way humans and machines communicate.

THE GOAL: ENHANCING HUMAN DECISION-MAKING

The ultimate aim of cognitive computing is not to replace human intelligence but to augment it. By simulating human thought processes, cognitive computing systems can assist in making sense of the overwhelming amount of data we are faced with daily, helping to uncover insights, suggest actions, and even predict outcomes. Whether it's in healthcare, finance, education, or any other field, cognitive computing has the potential to enhance human decision-making, providing a powerful tool to tackle complex problems with a level of speed and precision that complements human capabilities.

The journey into cognitive computing is an ongoing adventure, one that challenges our understanding of both computing and human cognition. As these systems become more sophisticated, they open up new possibilities for solving problems, creating innovations, and understanding our world. Yet, this journey also prompts important questions about ethics, privacy, and the nature of intelligence itself—questions that we must navigate carefully as we explore the vast potential of cognitive computing.

In essence, cognitive computing represents a bridge between human thought and machine processing, a fusion of the emotional and the algorithmic, that seeks to enhance our ability to understand and interact with the complex world around us. It's a testament to the human spirit of innovation and our enduring quest to expand the horizons of what technology can achieve.

FROM TURING TO TODAY

As we delve into the tapestry of artificial intelligence's rich history, our journey begins in the mid-20th century with a figure whose contributions laid the groundwork for what we now recognize as AI. Alan Turing, a British mathematician and logician, embarked on a quest that would forever alter our understanding of machine intelligence and computational thinking. His pioneering work not only cracked complex codes during World War II but also posed a question that remains central to AI philosophy: Can machines think?

ALAN TURING AND THE BIRTH OF COMPUTATIONAL THINKING

In 1950, Turing introduced the world to what is now known as the Turing Test through his seminal paper, "Computing Machinery and Intelligence." This test was a simple yet profound challenge: if a machine could engage in a conversation with a human, with the human unable to distinguish between the machine and another human being, then the machine could be said to exhibit intelligent behavior. Turing's test wasn't just about trickery or superficial imitation; it was about the essence of thought itself, challenging the very notion of what it means to think and understand.

THE TURING TEST: A BENCHMARK FOR INTELLIGENCE

The Turing Test set a benchmark for artificial intelligence that still captivates and challenges researchers today. It shifted the conversation from whether machines could calculate or perform specific tasks to whether they could emulate the depth and nuance of human interaction. This was a radical departure from the mechanical view of computation, proposing a future where machines could potentially possess qualities akin to human thought and consciousness.

THE EVOLUTION OF AI: MILESTONES AND INNOVATIONS

Following Turing's ground-breaking ideas, the field of AI began to take shape, marked by several key milestones:

The 1950s and 1960s: The Formative Years - This era saw the development of the first AI programs. Researchers like Allen Newell and Herbert A. Simon created Logic Theorist and General Problem Solver, programs that could solve puzzles and prove mathematical theorems, embodying Turing's vision of machine intelligence.

The 1970s: Expansion and Exploration - AI research expanded into new areas, including natural language processing and robotics. These years were characterized by both enthusiasm and challenges, as researchers confronted the limitations of technology and understanding.

The 1980s to the 1990s: The Rise of Machine Learning - A shift towards data-driven approaches marked this period. Machine learning emerged as a dominant paradigm, focusing on algorithms that could learn from and make predictions based on data, leading to significant advancements in pattern recognition and predictive analytics.

The 21st Century: AI Goes Mainstream - With the explosion of data and computational power, AI technologies have become an integral part of everyday life. From personal assistants like Siri and Alexa to breakthroughs in deep learning, AI's capabilities have expanded dramatically, touching every aspect of society.

A LEGACY THAT ENDURES

Alan Turing's legacy is a testament to the power of visionary thinking. His ideas laid the foundation for a field that continues to evolve, pushing the boundaries of what machines can do. From the Turing Test to the latest advancements in AI, the journey of artificial intelligence is a story of human curiosity, ingenuity, and the relentless pursuit of understanding the essence of intelligence itself.

As we stand on the shoulders of giants like Turing, we look towards a future where AI promises to redefine the limits of technology, creativity, and problem-solving. The history of AI, from Turing to today, is not just a chronicle of technological advancement but a reflection of our enduring quest to mirror and augment the human intellect through the power of machines.

KEY MILESTONES IN AI DEVELOPMENT

The odyssey of artificial intelligence (AI) is a saga of human ambition, ingenuity, and, at times, humility, as we've navigated both breakthroughs and setbacks. This journey is punctuated by key milestones that have shaped the development of AI, from its conceptual beginnings to its pervasive presence in today's digital world. Let's explore these pivotal moments that have defined the evolution of AI.

THE CREATION OF THE FIRST NEURAL NETWORK COMPUTER

In the late 1950s, a significant leap was made with the creation of the first neural network computer, the Mark I Perceptron, designed by Frank Rosenblatt. This machine was inspired by the workings of the human brain, albeit in a very rudimentary form. It was capable of learning and making decisions by adjusting the weights of its connections based on input data, a fundamental concept that underpins modern neural networks. The Perceptron sparked excitement about the potential for machines to learn from experience, setting the stage for the development of more sophisticated AI models.

THE DARTMOUTH CONFERENCE: THE BIRTH OF AI

The year 1956 marked the official birth of artificial intelligence as a distinct field of study, thanks to the Dartmouth Conference. Organized by John McCarthy, Marvin Minsky, Nathaniel Rochester, and Claude Shannon, this gathering was predicated on the belief that "every aspect of learning or any other feature of intelligence can in principle be so precisely described that a machine can be made to simulate it." This conference not only coined the term "artificial intelligence" but also ignited a flurry of research and investment in the field, establishing AI as a central pursuit in computer science.

THE AI WINTERS: PERIODS OF DISILLUSIONMENT

The journey of AI has not been without its valleys. The AI winters — periods in the 1970s and again in the late 1980s to early 1990s — were times of reduced funding and waning interest in AI research. These winters were precipitated by inflated expectations that led to disappointment when the technology failed to deliver on its promised potential, coupled with limitations in computational power and data availability. The first winter was largely due to the realization that early AI systems could not scale to solve real-world problems, while the second was triggered by the failure of machine translation and expert systems to achieve commercial viability.

THE RESURGENCE OF AI IN THE 21ST CENTURY

The 21st century has witnessed a remarkable resurgence in AI, fuelled by significant advances in computational power, the explosion of data, and breakthroughs in machine learning algorithms, particularly deep learning. The advent of GPUs (Graphics Processing Units) and improvements in storage and processing capabilities have enabled researchers to train larger neural networks, leading to unprecedented achievements in AI. This era has seen AI master complex games like Go, drive autonomous vehicles, revolutionize language translation, and personalize user experiences on digital platforms. AI is now a driving force behind innovations in healthcare, finance, entertainment, and beyond, marking its transition from academic curiosity to a transformative technology in society.

LOOKING FORWARD

As we reflect on these milestones, it's clear that the journey of AI is a testament to human curiosity and our relentless pursuit of knowledge. From the creation of the first neural network computer to the ground-breaking Dartmouth Conference, through the challenges of the AI winters, and onto the resurgence powered by today's technological advances, AI's history is rich with lessons and inspirations. As we stand on the brink of new discoveries and applications, the story of AI continues to evolve, promising to reshape our world in ways we are only beginning to imagine.

EVOLUTION OF AI TECHNOLOGIES AND METHODOLOGIES OVER THE YEARS

The evolution of artificial intelligence (AI) technologies and methodologies over the years is a captivating narrative of innovation, adaptation, and breakthroughs. This journey from rule-based systems to the sophisticated realms of machine learning and deep learning reflects our growing understanding of intelligence, learning, and the potential for machines to mimic, complement, and enhance human capabilities.

RULE-BASED SYSTEMS: THE EARLY DAYS

The inception of AI was dominated by rule-based systems, also known as expert systems, in the 1960s and 1970s. These systems operated on a straightforward principle: human experts encoded their knowledge into a set of explicit rules that machines could follow to make decisions or solve problems. For example, if a patient has symptom X, then consider diagnosis Y. This approach allowed machines to perform tasks that required human-like reasoning within specific domains, such as medical diagnosis or playing chess.

However, rule-based systems had their limitations. They struggled with tasks that required understanding of context or nuance, and they couldn't learn from new data. The complexity and cost of manually coding all possible rules for a domain also became prohibitive as the ambition of AI grew. This realization prompted the search for more flexible, adaptive approaches to AI.

THE SHIFT TO MACHINE LEARNING

The limitations of rule-based systems led to the emergence of machine learning in the 1980s and 1990s, marking a significant shift in the AI landscape. Machine learning focuses on developing algorithms that allow computers to learn from and make predictions or decisions based on data. Instead of being explicitly programmed with rules, machine learning systems learn the rules themselves by identifying patterns in data.

This shift was revolutionary. It opened up new possibilities for AI applications, from email spam filters and recommendation systems to speech recognition and image classification. Machine learning also introduced a variety of approaches, including decision trees, support vector machines, and ensemble methods like random forests, each with its strengths and suited to different types of problems.

THE RISE OF NEURAL NETWORKS AND DEEP LEARNING

While neural networks—a type of machine learning inspired by the structure and function of the human brain—were explored early in AI's history, they came to the forefront with the advent of deep learning in the 2000s. Deep learning involves neural networks with many layers (hence "deep") that can learn increasingly abstract representations of data. This capability has led to breakthroughs in fields that were once considered challenging for AI, such as natural language processing, computer vision, and complex game playing.

Deep learning's success is largely attributed to the availability of large datasets and significant increases in computational power, particularly through the use of GPUs. These advancements have enabled the training of deep neural networks that can learn from vast amounts of unstructured data, from images and text to audio and video.

FROM DEEP LEARNING TO AI TODAY

Today, AI technologies and methodologies continue to evolve at a rapid pace. Deep learning remains at the forefront, driving innovations like generative adversarial networks (GANs) for creating realistic images and transformers for understanding and generating human language. Meanwhile, the field is also exploring new paradigms, such as reinforcement learning, where AI systems learn to make decisions by interacting with their environment, and few-shot learning, which aims to reduce the amount of data needed to train AI models.

The evolution from rule-based systems to machine learning and deep learning reflects the dynamic nature of AI research and development. As we push the boundaries of what AI can achieve, we also revisit and refine older methodologies, integrating them with new insights and technologies. This iterative, expanding exploration of AI continues to transform our world, promising even more profound changes in the decades to come.

NARROW AI VS. GENERAL AI

In the kaleidoscopic world of artificial intelligence (AI), the technologies we develop fall into two broad categories that reflect their capabilities and potential: Narrow AI (also known as Weak AI) and General AI (also referred to as Strong AI). These distinctions are not just academic; they fundamentally shape our understanding of AI's current abilities and its future trajectory.

NARROW AI: MASTERY OF SPECIFIC TASKS

Narrow AI is the type of artificial intelligence that is prevalent today. It is designed to perform a specific task or a set of closely related tasks with a high degree of competence, often surpassing human performance in those specific domains. However, the key characteristic of Narrow AI is its limitations; it operates under a predefined range or context and cannot perform beyond its programming or training.

EXAMPLES OF NARROW AI INCLUDE:

Personal Assistants: Siri, Alexa, and Google Assistant can understand and respond to voice commands, set reminders, or play music, but their capabilities are confined to predefined tasks.

Image Recognition Systems: These systems can identify and classify objects within images with remarkable accuracy, used in everything from tagging photos on social media to diagnosing diseases from medical imaging.

Recommendation Systems: The algorithms behind Netflix's movie suggestions or Amazon's product recommendations are adept at predicting what you might like based on your past behaviour and the behaviour of others, but their expertise does not extend beyond making these recommendations.

Narrow AI systems are powered by machine learning algorithms and, in many cases, deep learning, allowing them to improve their performance as they are exposed to more data within their specific task domain. However, they lack the ability to generalize their intelligence to tasks or domains they weren't specifically designed for.

GENERAL AI: THE QUEST FOR HUMAN-LIKE INTELLIGENCE

General AI, on the other hand, remains a theoretical concept and a goal for future AI research. It refers to an AI system's ability to understand, learn, and apply its intelligence to any problem, much like a human being. Unlike Narrow AI, General AI would possess the ability to transfer knowledge and learning from one domain to another, demonstrating a form of understanding and consciousness that allows it to perform any intellectual task that a human can.

While General AI does not yet exist, its envisioned capabilities might include:

Adaptive Learning and Reasoning: A General AI system could learn new languages, solve complex mathematical problems, and write poetry or music, all with minimal human input.

Common Sense and Decision Making: It would possess the kind of common sense that humans take for granted, such as understanding that water is wet without needing to be explicitly told or experiencing it.

Emotional Intelligence: Beyond logical reasoning, General AI would ideally understand and interpret human emotions, potentially responding in a way that reflects empathy and emotional awareness.

THE DISTINCTIONS AND THEIR IMPLICATIONS

The distinction between Narrow AI and General AI is not just about their current capabilities but also about the philosophical and technical challenges each presents. Narrow AI, while incredibly powerful within its domain, does not aspire to replicate human intelligence in its entirety. It is a tool, albeit a sophisticated one, designed to enhance human capabilities in specific areas.

General AI, with its goal of mimicking human intelligence, raises profound questions about the nature of consciousness, ethics, and the future relationship between humans and machines. The development of General AI would represent a seismic shift in AI research and our understanding of intelligence itself, with implications that are difficult to fully predict.

As we continue to advance in the field of AI, the journey from Narrow AI to the potential realization of General AI encapsulates both our technological ambitions and the philosophical inquiries that accompany our quest to understand and replicate the essence of human intelligence.

CURRENT STATE OF AI TECHNOLOGY

In today's technological landscape, artificial intelligence (AI) has woven itself into the fabric of our daily lives, often in ways that are invisible yet impactful. The current state of AI technology is predominantly characterized by Narrow AI, systems designed to excel in specific tasks or domains, demonstrating remarkable capabilities that can sometimes surpass human expertise. This form of AI, also known as Weak AI, has become a cornerstone of modern innovation, driving advancements across various sectors including healthcare, finance, entertainment, and transportation.

THE PREVALENCE OF NARROW AI

Narrow AI is everywhere, from the virtual assistants in our smartphones to the sophisticated algorithms that filter our email inboxes, curate our social media feeds, and recommend movies or products tailored to our preferences. These systems are highly specialized, trained on vast datasets to perform particular tasks with incredible accuracy and efficiency. For instance:

Facial Recognition: Used in security systems and smartphones, facial recognition technology can identify or verify a person from a digital image or video frame. This technology relies on Narrow AI to analyze facial features and match them with images in a database with high precision.

Internet Searches: Search engines use AI to understand and rank billions of webpages based on relevance to user queries. These algorithms have become adept at interpreting the intent behind our searches, delivering results that are increasingly personalized and accurate.

Autonomous Vehicles: Self-driving cars combine various AI technologies, including image recognition, sensor processing, and predictive modelling, to navigate safely. Each of these tasks requires AI systems that are finely tuned to handle specific aspects of driving, from detecting pedestrians to predicting the actions of other vehicles.

THE CAPABILITIES AND LIMITATIONS OF NARROW AI

The strength of Narrow AI lies in its ability to process and analyze data at a scale and speed that humans cannot match, leading to improvements in efficiency, accuracy, and productivity. However, it's important to recognize the inherent limitations of these systems. Narrow AI operates within the confines of its programming and training data; it lacks the ability to generalize its intelligence across unrelated tasks or to adapt to new, unforeseen scenarios in the way humans can. For example, an AI trained to diagnose skin cancer from images cannot leverage its learning to understand traffic patterns or financial markets.

THE FUTURE TRAJECTORY OF AI TECHNOLOGY

As we look to the future, the evolution of AI technology is likely to see enhancements in the capabilities of Narrow AI, with systems becoming more sophisticated, accurate, and integrated into various aspects of human life. The development of more advanced machine learning techniques, such as few-shot learning and transfer learning, aims to address some of the limitations of Narrow AI, enabling systems to learn from fewer examples and apply knowledge across different tasks more effectively.

The quest for General AI, a system that can understand, learn, and apply its intelligence to any intellectual task, remains a long-term goal. Achieving General AI would mark a monumental shift in AI technology, but it also raises complex ethical, social, and philosophical questions about the role of intelligent machines in society.

CONCLUSION

In summary, the current state of AI technology is dominated by Narrow AI, systems that are transforming industries and daily life with their task-specific intelligence. While these advancements are impressive, they represent only the initial steps toward the broader aspirations of AI. As we continue to push the boundaries of what AI can achieve, the journey ahead promises to be both exciting and challenging, with the potential to redefine our relationship with technology.

CONCEPT OF GENERAL AI

The concept of General AI, or Strong AI, represents a future where machines possess the ability to perform any intellectual task that a human being can. Unlike Narrow AI, which is designed for specific tasks, General AI would have the capacity for understanding, reasoning, learning, and even consciousness akin to human intelligence. This vision of AI not only pushes the boundaries of technology but also invites us to reimagine the essence of intelligence, creativity, and decision-making. As we explore the potential of General AI, it's crucial to consider not only the technological advancements it promises but also the profound ethical and societal implications it entails.

General AI could revolutionize every aspect of human life and society. Its potential applications are vast and varied, including:

Scientific Discovery: General AI could accelerate research in fields such as physics, chemistry, and biology, solving complex problems faster than human scientists and potentially unlocking new frontiers in knowledge.

Healthcare: With the ability to understand and diagnose any medical condition, General AI could offer personalized treatment plans, manage healthcare systems, and even perform surgeries, significantly improving patient outcomes.

Education: Tailored learning experiences could be created for each student, adapting in real-time to their needs, pace, and learning style, potentially transforming the educational landscape.

Economic and Social Planning: General AI could optimize resource allocation, predict and mitigate crises, and help design more equitable and sustainable societies.

ETHICAL CONSIDERATIONS

The development of General AI raises several ethical considerations that must be addressed to ensure the technology benefits humanity while minimizing risks:

Autonomy and Control: As machines approach human-level intelligence, ensuring they remain aligned with human values and intentions becomes increasingly challenging. The risk of AI systems making decisions contrary to human welfare or ethical standards raises concerns about autonomy, control, and safety.

Privacy: With AI systems capable of understanding and processing vast amounts of personal data, safeguarding individual privacy becomes paramount. Ensuring that AI respects privacy rights and uses data ethically is a significant challenge.

Bias and Fairness: AI systems learn from data, which can reflect historical biases. General AI could perpetuate or even exacerbate these biases if not carefully designed and monitored, affecting fairness in decision-making processes across society.

The advent of General AI would also have profound societal implications, including:

Employment and the Economy: While General AI could create new opportunities and industries, it could also automate jobs across sectors, from manual labour to cognitive tasks, raising questions about employment, income distribution, and economic inequality.

Education and Skills: Preparing for a world with General AI requires rethinking education and skills development, emphasizing creativity, critical thinking, and emotional intelligence to complement AI's capabilities.

Governance and Regulation: The development and deployment of General AI necessitate robust governance frameworks to ensure its benefits are widely distributed and its risks are managed. This includes international cooperation to address global challenges and opportunities presented by AI.

CONCLUSION

The concept of General AI invites us to envision a future where machines not only augment human abilities but also potentially possess their own form of intelligence. While the technological achievements of General AI could be transformative, realizing this future responsibly requires careful consideration of the ethical and societal implications. Balancing the promise of General AI with the need to safeguard human values, rights, and welfare is one of the most significant challenges of the 21st century, demanding a collaborative approach among technologists, ethicists, policymakers, and the broader public. As we stand on the brink of this new frontier, the choices we make today will shape the trajectory of AI and its impact on society for generations to come.

CHAPTER 2: HOW AI WORKS: AN OVERVIEW

THE FUEL OF AI

In the realm of artificial intelligence (AI), data plays the starring role, acting as the indispensable fuel that powers these advanced systems. Just as a car needs gasoline to run, AI systems require data to operate, learn, and make decisions. But what makes data so crucial for AI, and how do different types of data affect AI systems? Let's delve into these questions, exploring the essence of data's role in AI, the distinction between structured and unstructured data, and the paramount importance of data quality.

THE CENTRAL ROLE OF DATA IN AI

At its core, AI involves creating algorithms that process information and make decisions or predictions based on that information. This process is akin to learning, where the algorithm, through exposure to data, identifies patterns, infers relationships, and improves its performance over time. Data, therefore, is not just a resource but the very foundation upon which AI systems build their understanding and capabilities. Without data, AI cannot "learn," and without learning, there is no AI.

TYPES OF DATA: STRUCTURED VS. UNSTRUCTURED

AI systems can consume and process various types of data, broadly categorized into structured and unstructured forms:

Structured Data: This type of data is highly organized and formatted in a way that makes it easily searchable and understandable by AI algorithms. Structured data typically resides in relational databases or spreadsheets, where it is arranged into rows and columns with defined data types. Examples include customer names, addresses, transaction dates, and prices. Structured data is akin to a neatly organized library, where every book has a specific place and can be easily located.

Unstructured Data: In contrast, unstructured data is not organized in a predefined manner and comes in various formats, making it more challenging for AI systems to process. This category includes text documents, emails, social media posts, videos, images, and audio files. Unstructured data is like a vast attic filled with an assortment of items, each requiring individual assessment to understand its content and value.

The ability of AI systems to handle unstructured data has significantly advanced in recent years, especially with the development of natural language processing (NLP) and computer vision technologies. These advancements have opened up vast new territories for AI applications, from understanding human speech to recognizing objects in images.

WHY DATA QUALITY MATTERS

The adage "garbage in, garbage out" is particularly apt when it comes to AI. The quality of the data fed into AI systems directly impacts their effectiveness and reliability. High-quality data is accurate, complete, relevant, and timely, enabling AI algorithms to learn correctly and perform their tasks effectively. Conversely, poor-quality data can lead to inaccurate predictions, flawed decision-making, and, ultimately, a loss of trust in AI systems.

SEVERAL FACTORS CONTRIBUTE TO DATA QUALITY, INCLUDING:

Accuracy: The data must accurately represent the real-world entities or events it is supposed to depict.

Completeness: Missing values or incomplete data records can skew AI learning and analysis.

Consistency: Data collected from different sources should maintain consistency to avoid confusing AI algorithms.

Relevance: The data must be relevant to the specific problem or task the AI system is designed to address.

Timeliness: Outdated data can lead to decisions that are no longer applicable or effective.

Ensuring data quality is an ongoing challenge that requires rigorous data management practices, including regular cleaning, validation, and updating of data sets. As AI continues to evolve and integrate into various aspects of life and work, the importance of high-quality data as the fuel for AI becomes ever more critical, underpinning the reliability, effectiveness, and trustworthiness of AI systems.

PROCESS OF COLLECTING AND PREPARING DATA FOR AI

The journey of an AI system from conception to implementation is paved with numerous critical steps, among which the collection and preparation of data stand out as foundational. This process is akin to preparing the soil and sowing the seeds for a garden; just as the quality of the soil and the care in planting determine the health of the plants, the meticulous collection and preparation of data determine the effectiveness and efficiency of AI systems. Let's delve into this process, emphasizing the importance of data cleaning, normalization, and augmentation.

COLLECTING DATA

The first step in the data preparation process is collection. Data can be sourced from a myriad of origins, including internal databases, online repositories, sensors, and interactions with users. The goal is to gather a comprehensive dataset that accurately represents the problem space the AI is intended to address. This phase requires careful planning to ensure the data is relevant, diverse, and sufficient in volume to train robust AI models.

CHALLENGES IN DATA COLLECTION:

Ensuring diversity to avoid bias.
Guaranteeing the data's relevance to the task.
Navigating privacy and ethical considerations, especially with personal data.

PREPARING DATA

Once collected, the raw data often resembles a rough diamond that needs cutting and polishing to reveal its value. This preparation phase involves several key processes:

DATA CLEANING

Data cleaning is the process of detecting and correcting (or removing) corrupt or inaccurate records from a dataset. This step is crucial because errors, outliers, or missing values can significantly distort the learning process of AI models, leading to inaccurate outcomes.

Techniques include: Identifying outliers, filling in missing values, and correcting inconsistencies.

Importance: Clean data ensures the reliability of AI predictions and decisions, directly impacting the system's effectiveness.

NORMALIZATION

Normalization involves scaling numeric data values to a standard range or distribution. This step is particularly important when different features have different scales and ranges, as it ensures that no single feature dominates the learning process due to its scale.

Techniques include: Scaling features to a range between 0 and 1 or transforming them to have a mean of 0 and a standard deviation of 1.

Importance: Normalized data facilitates faster and more stable convergence during the training of AI models, improving the learning efficiency.

DATA AUGMENTATION

Data augmentation is a technique used to increase the diversity of data available for training models without actually collecting new data. This is especially useful in domains like image and speech recognition, where acquiring labelled data can be expensive and time-consuming.

Techniques include: For images, augmentation might involve rotations, flipping, or varying the lighting conditions. For text, it might involve synonym replacement or sentence restructuring.

Importance: Augmentation can significantly enhance the robustness of AI models, making them more capable of handling real-world variability and reducing overfitting.

THE IMPACT OF QUALITY DATA PREPARATION

The meticulous preparation of data—through cleaning, normalization, and augmentation—lays the groundwork for the development of effective and reliable AI systems. This process not only enhances the performance of AI models but also contributes to their fairness and transparency by mitigating biases and ensuring a level playing field across different data features.

Moreover, quality data preparation is an iterative and ongoing process. As AI systems interact with the real world, they encounter new data, which may necessitate revisiting and refining the preparation steps to maintain or improve the system's performance.

In conclusion, the collection and preparation of data are critical stages in the AI development process, requiring careful attention to detail and a deep understanding of the problem domain. By ensuring the cleanliness, normalization, and augmentation of data, AI practitioners can significantly increase the chances of their systems succeeding in the complex and ever-changing real world.

ETHICAL CONSIDERATIONS IN DATA COLLECTION

The ethical considerations in data collection for artificial intelligence (AI) are paramount, touching on issues that affect not only the integrity and performance of AI systems but also the broader societal implications of their deployment. As AI technologies become increasingly integrated into various aspects of daily life, the way data is collected, processed, and used raises significant ethical questions, particularly regarding privacy, bias, and the potential for harm. Let's explore these considerations in more detail.

PRIVACY CONCERNS

Privacy stands at the forefront of ethical considerations in AI data collection. With the vast amounts of personal information being harvested—ranging from online behaviour to biometric data—the potential for privacy infringement is high. Ethical data collection practices must respect individual privacy rights and comply with regulations such as the General Data Protection Regulation (GDPR) in Europe.

Consent and Transparency: Individuals should be fully informed about what data is being collected, for what purpose, and how it will be used, with explicit consent obtained where necessary.

Data Minimization: Collecting only the data that is directly necessary for the specified purpose can help mitigate privacy risks.

Anonymization and Pseudonymization: Techniques that anonymize or pseudonymize data can protect individual identities, though they are not fool proof against re-identification in some cases.

BIAS IN DATA SETS

Bias in data collection is another critical ethical issue. Data sets can reflect existing prejudices in society, whether through the underrepresentation of certain groups or the perpetuation of stereotypes. When AI systems are trained on biased data, they can amplify these biases, leading to unfair or discriminatory outcomes.

Diverse and Representative Data: Ensuring data sets are diverse and representative of the population is crucial to mitigate bias. This involves actively seeking out data from underrepresented groups and considering the context in which data is collected.

Bias Detection and Correction: Ongoing efforts to detect and correct biases in data sets are essential. This can involve statistical analysis to identify disparities and the development of algorithms designed to counteract bias.

IMPACT OF BIASED DATA ON AI PERFORMANCE

The impact of biased data on AI performance cannot be overstated. AI systems trained on biased data can produce outcomes that are not only unfair but also inaccurate for certain groups of people. This undermines the reliability and trustworthiness of AI applications, from facial recognition technology and hiring algorithms to healthcare diagnostics and predictive policing.

Unfair Treatment: Biased data can lead AI systems to treat individuals or groups unfairly, such as by denying them opportunities or services based on biased criteria.

Erosion of Trust: The use of biased AI systems can erode public trust in technology and institutions, particularly if they consistently produce discriminatory outcomes.

Legal and Reputational Risks: Organizations deploying AI systems risk legal challenges and reputational damage if their systems are found to be biased or discriminatory.

MOVING FORWARD

Addressing the ethical considerations in data collection for AI requires a multifaceted approach:

Ethical Guidelines and Standards: Developing and adhering to ethical guidelines and standards for data collection and AI development is crucial. This includes principles of fairness, accountability, transparency, and respect for human rights.

Regulatory Compliance: Complying with existing regulations and advocating for the development of new laws that address the unique challenges of AI ethics and data privacy.

Stakeholder Engagement: Engaging with stakeholders, including affected communities, ethicists, and regulators, can provide diverse perspectives and help identify potential ethical issues early in the AI development process.

In conclusion, the ethical considerations in data collection for AI are complex and multifaceted, requiring ongoing attention and action from all stakeholders involved in AI development. By prioritizing privacy, actively combating bias, and addressing the potential impacts of biased data, the AI community can work towards the responsible and ethical use of technology that benefits society as a whole.

ALGORITHMS: THE BUILDING BLOCKS OF AI

Imagine you're following a recipe to bake a cake. The recipe provides you with a list of ingredients and a series of steps that guide you through mixing those ingredients, setting the oven temperature, and baking for a certain amount of time until the cake is done. In this analogy, the recipe acts like an algorithm for baking a cake. Similarly, in the world of artificial intelligence (AI), algorithms are the recipes that guide AI systems on how to process data and make decisions, solve problems, or perform tasks.

WHAT IS AN ALGORITHM?

An algorithm is a set of step-by-step instructions or rules designed to perform a specific task or solve a particular problem. In AI, these algorithms are like the brain's thought processes, enabling machines to learn from data, recognize patterns, and make decisions with minimal human intervention. Algorithms can range from simple formulas to complex sets of instructions that adapt and change as they are exposed to more data.

EXAMPLES OF AI ALGORITHMS

Sorting Algorithms: Consider the task of organizing a bookshelf. A sorting algorithm in AI works similarly by arranging data into a specified order, such as sorting email messages by date or prioritizing tasks based on urgency.

Search Algorithms: Imagine playing a game of hide and seek. A search algorithm helps an AI system find information or an item from within a dataset efficiently, akin to how you might strategize to find your friends based on clues. Machine Learning Algorithms: Think of learning to ride a bike. Initially, you adjust your balance based on how you feel when you lean too much to one side or the other. Machine learning algorithms adjust predictions based on feedback, learning over time to improve accuracy, much like you learn to maintain balance.

THE ROLE OF ALGORITHMS IN AI

Algorithms are the foundation upon which AI systems are built and operate. They play a crucial role in:

Data Processing: Algorithms help AI systems to process and analyze vast amounts of data, identifying patterns and insights that would be impossible for humans to discern quickly.

Decision Making: AI algorithms can evaluate different options and make decisions based on predefined criteria, from recommending a movie on a streaming platform to autonomously driving a car.

Learning and Adaptation: Through machine learning algorithms, AI systems can learn from new data, adapt their strategies, and improve their performance over time without being explicitly reprogrammed.

THE IMPORTANCE OF ALGORITHM DESIGN

The design of an AI algorithm determines how effectively and efficiently it can perform its task. A well-designed algorithm can process data accurately and quickly, leading to better decision-making and more intelligent behaviour from AI systems. Conversely, a poorly designed algorithm might be inefficient, slow, or prone to errors, which can undermine the performance of the AI system.

Designing effective AI algorithms requires a deep understanding of both the problem being solved and the characteristics of the data being used. It also involves selecting the right algorithmic approach, whether it's a simple decision tree or a complex neural network, and fine-tuning it to optimize performance.

CONCLUSION

Algorithms are the building blocks of AI, providing the instructions and processes that enable machines to perform tasks that require intelligence. Just as a recipe guides you through baking a cake, algorithms guide AI systems through processing data, making decisions, and learning from experiences. As we continue to advance in the field of AI, the development of innovative and efficient algorithms remains a key focus, driving the evolution of intelligent systems capable of transforming the world in myriad ways.

DIFFERENT TYPES OF AI ALGORITHMS

Artificial Intelligence (AI) algorithms are the engines that power AI systems, enabling them to perform tasks that typically require human intelligence. These algorithms can be broadly categorized into several types, each with its unique principles and applications. Let's delve into three fundamental categories: rule-based algorithms, machine learning models, and evolutionary algorithms.

RULE-BASED ALGORITHMS

Basic Principles: Rule-based algorithms operate on a set of predefined rules or conditions to make decisions. These rules are explicitly programmed by humans based on knowledge of the domain. The algorithm evaluates input data against these rules to determine the output or action. The process is somewhat akin to a flowchart where each decision leads to a specific outcome based on logical conditions.

Applications: Rule-based systems are widely used in expert systems, where they help in decision-making processes by simulating the reasoning that an expert might use to reach a conclusion. They are prevalent in domains with clear, well-defined rules, such as legal compliance checks, tax calculations, or medical diagnosis systems where the input data and the decision criteria are straightforward and well understood.

MACHINE LEARNING MODELS

Basic Principles: Machine learning (ML) models differ significantly from rule-based systems. Instead of relying on predefined rules, ML algorithms learn the rules from the data. By processing large datasets, these algorithms identify patterns and relationships within the data and learn to make predictions or decisions based on those learnings. There are several types of machine learning, including supervised learning (learning from labelled data), unsupervised learning (finding hidden patterns in data), and reinforcement learning (learning based on feedback from interactions with the environment).

Applications: Machine learning models have a vast range of applications across industries. In finance, they're used for credit scoring and algorithmic trading. In healthcare, they assist in disease diagnosis and personalized medicine. In the tech industry, ML models power recommendation systems for platforms like Netflix and Spotify, and they're behind the advancements in natural language processing seen in virtual assistants like Siri and Alexa.

EVOLUTIONARY ALGORITHMS

Basic Principles: Evolutionary algorithms are inspired by the process of natural selection and genetics. These algorithms simulate a process of evolution to solve optimization and search problems. They start with a set of candidate solutions and iteratively evolve these solutions by applying operations analogous to biological processes, such as mutation, crossover (recombination), and selection. Over generations, the population of solutions evolves toward an optimal or satisfactory solution.

Applications: Evolutionary algorithms are particularly useful for solving complex optimization problems where traditional approaches might be inefficient or infeasible. They have been successfully applied in areas such as scheduling, where they optimize the allocation of resources; in engineering design, to find optimal designs for structures or materials; and in robotics, for evolving behaviours or control strategies for autonomous robots.

CONCLUSION

The diversity of AI algorithms—from rule-based systems with their clear and logical frameworks, through the adaptive and predictive power of machine learning models, to the innovative and exploratory nature of evolutionary algorithms—highlights the breadth and depth of AI's capabilities. Each type of algorithm has its strengths and ideal use cases, and understanding these can help developers and researchers choose the most appropriate approach for their specific AI challenges. As the field of AI continues to evolve, we can expect the development of even more sophisticated algorithms, further expanding the potential applications and impact of AI technology.

CHALLENGES IN DESIGNING AI ALGORITHMS

Designing AI algorithms is a complex endeavour that involves balancing accuracy, efficiency, and fairness, among other factors. These challenges are at the forefront of AI research and development, with ongoing efforts aimed at overcoming them. Let's delve into these challenges and explore the strategies being employed to address them.

ENSURING ACCURACY

Challenge: Achieving high accuracy is crucial for AI algorithms, especially in applications where decisions have significant consequences, such as healthcare diagnosis, financial forecasting, and autonomous driving. However, ensuring accuracy can be difficult due to issues like overfitting, where the model performs well on training data but poorly on unseen data, and underfitting, where the model is too simple to capture the underlying pattern.

Ongoing Efforts:
Advanced Modelling Techniques: Researchers are continually developing more sophisticated models that can capture complex patterns in data without overfitting.

Data Augmentation: Increasing the diversity and amount of training data through techniques like synthetic data generation helps improve the model's generalization capabilities.

Regularization Techniques: Methods like dropout for neural networks or penalization techniques for regression models help prevent overfitting by adding constraints to the model.

ENHANCING EFFICIENCY

Challenge: AI algorithms, especially deep learning models, can be computationally intensive and require significant resources, making them less accessible for real-time applications or deployment on devices with limited processing power, like smartphones or IoT devices.

Ongoing Efforts:
Model Optimization: Techniques such as pruning (removing unnecessary weights) and quantization (reducing the precision of the weights) help reduce the size of AI models without significantly impacting performance.

Efficient Architectures: Researchers are designing new neural network architectures that require fewer computations, such as MobileNets and EfficientNets, which are optimized for mobile devices.

Edge Computing: Moving computation from the cloud to the edge (closer to where data is generated) reduces latency and bandwidth use, enhancing efficiency.

ENSURING FAIRNESS

Challenge: AI algorithms can perpetuate or even exacerbate biases present in their training data, leading to unfair outcomes. This is particularly concerning in applications like hiring, lending, and law enforcement, where biased decisions can have serious implications for individuals' lives.

Ongoing Efforts:
Bias Detection and Mitigation: Developing tools and methodologies to detect bias in datasets and model predictions is an active area of research. Techniques to mitigate bias include re-sampling training data, adjusting model outputs, and designing algorithms that are inherently more fair.

Inclusive Data Collection: Efforts to ensure that training data is representative of all groups can help reduce bias. This includes actively seeking out data from underrepresented groups and considering the context in which data is collected. Transparency and Explainability: Making AI systems more transparent and their decisions more explainable can help identify and correct biases. Techniques such as model interpretability tools and transparent reporting of model performance across different groups are key to these efforts.

CONCLUSION

The challenges of ensuring accuracy, efficiency, and fairness in AI algorithms are significant, but they are matched by the ingenuity and determination of the AI research community. Through a combination of advanced techniques, innovative approaches, and a commitment to ethical principles, ongoing efforts aim to overcome these challenges, pushing the boundaries of what AI can achieve while ensuring its benefits are equitably distributed. As AI continues to evolve, addressing these challenges head-on will be crucial for realizing its full potential in a way that is beneficial and fair for all.

MACHINE LEARNING AND DEEP LEARNING EXPLAINED

THE CONCEPT OF MACHINE LEARNING (ML)

Machine Learning (ML) and Deep Learning represent transformative facets of Artificial Intelligence (AI) that have reshaped our approach to data analysis, decision-making, and problem-solving. At their core, these technologies enable machines to learn from data, making sense of the world in a way that mimics human learning to some extent. Let's break down these concepts, starting with machine learning, to understand how they empower computers to learn and improve over time.

MACHINE LEARNING: THE FOUNDATION

Machine Learning is a subset of AI focused on building algorithms that enable computers to learn from and make predictions or decisions based on data. Unlike traditional programming, where a developer writes explicit instructions to perform a task, ML allows a system to learn and make decisions from data, improving its accuracy over time as it processes more information.

HOW MACHINE LEARNING WORKS:

1. Learning from Data: At the heart of ML is the ability to learn from data. This process begins with feeding the machine learning model a dataset, which includes both the input data and the expected output. For example, in a spam detection system, the dataset would consist of numerous email messages along with labels indicating whether each email is "spam" or "not spam."

2. Model Training: The model learns by adjusting its parameters to minimize the difference between its predictions and the actual outcomes in the training data. This process is akin to a person learning to distinguish between different types of plants by repeatedly comparing their observations with a correct reference until their predictions become accurate.

3. Making Predictions: Once trained, the ML model can make predictions on new, unseen data. For instance, it can predict whether a new email message is spam based on the patterns it learned during training.

4. Feedback and Improvement: The model's performance can be evaluated using new data, and feedback from this evaluation can be used to refine the model, making it more accurate over time.

TYPES OF MACHINE LEARNING:

Supervised Learning: The model learns from a labelled dataset, trying to predict the output from the input data. Applications include image recognition and credit scoring.

Unsupervised Learning: The model learns from unlabelled data, trying to find inherent patterns or groupings in the data. Examples include customer segmentation and anomaly detection.

Reinforcement Learning: The model learns to make decisions by performing actions in an environment and receiving feedback in the form of rewards or penalties. It's used in robotics and game playing.

DEEP LEARNING: A SPECIALIZED SUBSET

Deep Learning is a specialized subset of machine learning that uses neural networks with many layers (hence "deep") to model complex patterns in data. Inspired by the structure and function of the human brain, deep learning models can learn from vast amounts of data at a level of complexity and abstraction that was previously unattainable.

HOW DEEP LEARNING ENHANCES MACHINE LEARNING:

Handling Unstructured Data: Deep learning excels at working with unstructured data such as images, audio, and text, making it possible to tackle a wide range of tasks from natural language processing to computer vision.

Automatic Feature Extraction: Unlike traditional ML models that require manual feature selection, deep learning models automatically discover the features to be used for learning, significantly simplifying the model development process.

Scalability and Performance: Deep learning models tend to improve as the amount of data increases, making them well-suited for today's data-rich world. They have achieved state-of-the-art performance in many areas, including speech recognition, language translation, and object detection.

CONCLUSION

Machine learning and deep learning represent ground-breaking approaches to AI, enabling computers to learn from data and improve over time. By automating the process of learning and decision-making, these technologies are driving innovations across numerous fields, transforming the way we interact with the world and paving the way for future advancements in AI.

DEEP LEARNING

Deep learning, a subfield of machine learning, has revolutionized the way machines understand and interpret the world around us. At the heart of deep learning is a structure inspired by the human brain itself: the neural network. These networks have layers of neurons—simple computational units that work together to process, analyze, and make predictions from data. Let's dive deeper into the structure of neural networks and explore why they are particularly powerful for tasks such as image recognition, natural language processing (NLP), and beyond.

STRUCTURE OF NEURAL NETWORKS

A neural network consists of an input layer, one or more hidden layers, and an output layer. Each layer is made up of nodes, or "neurons," which are connected by edges that carry weights.

Input Layer: This is where the neural network receives its data. Each node in the input layer represents a feature of the data. For example, in image recognition, each input node might represent a pixel's intensity.

Hidden Layers: These layers perform the bulk of the computation. As data passes through the hidden layers, the network identifies and extracts features. Early layers might detect simple patterns, like edges in an image, while deeper layers can identify more complex features, like shapes or objects. The "deep" in deep learning refers to networks with many hidden layers, enabling the extraction of high-level features from raw data.

Output Layer: This layer produces the final prediction or classification based on the features extracted by the hidden layers. For instance, in image recognition, the output layer would identify the object present in the image.

WHY NEURAL NETWORKS EXCEL AT COMPLEX TASKS

ABILITY TO HANDLE HIGH-DIMENSIONAL DATA

Neural networks are adept at processing data with many features, such as high-resolution images or lengthy text documents. Their structure allows them to manage the complexity and interconnectivity of such data, making sense of information that would be intractable for humans or traditional algorithms.

FEATURE EXTRACTION AND REPRESENTATION LEARNING

One of the most powerful aspects of deep learning is its ability to automatically discover and learn the most relevant features for a given task. This automatic feature extraction is a significant departure from traditional machine learning, where feature selection and engineering are performed manually. In tasks like image recognition, this means a neural network can learn to identify features such as edges, textures, and shapes without being explicitly programmed to look for them.

Flexibility and Adaptability

Deep learning models are highly adaptable. The same basic architecture, such as a convolutional neural network (CNN) for image tasks or a recurrent neural network (RNN) for sequential data, can be applied to a wide range of problems within their domain. This versatility makes deep learning a valuable tool across diverse fields, from medical diagnosis to autonomous driving.

APPLICATIONS IN IMAGE RECOGNITION AND NATURAL LANGUAGE PROCESSING

Image Recognition: Deep learning shines in image recognition tasks. CNNs, a type of neural network designed to process pixel data, are particularly effective. They can identify patterns and objects in images with remarkable accuracy, powering applications from facial recognition to medical imaging analysis.

Natural Language Processing (NLP): Deep learning has also transformed NLP, enabling machines to understand, interpret, and generate human language with unprecedented sophistication. Models like transformers have achieved state-of-the-art results in translation, text summarization, and question-answering systems by effectively capturing the context and nuances of language.

CONCLUSION

Deep learning, through its neural network architecture, has become a cornerstone of modern AI, enabling significant advances in image recognition, NLP, and beyond. Its ability to process complex, high-dimensional data, learn features automatically, and adapt to a wide range of tasks makes it a powerful tool for tackling some of the most challenging problems in computer science and beyond. As research in deep learning continues to advance, we can expect even more innovative applications and improvements in the ability of machines to understand and interact with the world around them.

EXAMPLES OF REAL-WORLD APPLICATIONS

Machine learning (ML) and deep learning, subsets of artificial intelligence (AI), are revolutionizing industries and impacting our daily lives in myriad ways. From enhancing customer experiences to advancing scientific research, these technologies are at the forefront of digital innovation. Here are several examples of real-world applications that highlight how ML and deep learning are transforming various sectors.

HEALTHCARE

Disease Diagnosis and Imaging: Deep learning models, particularly convolutional neural networks (CNNs), are being used to analyze medical images, such as X-rays and MRIs, with high accuracy. These models can detect anomalies and diseases, such as cancer, often earlier or more reliably than human practitioners. For instance, Google Health developed an AI model that can detect breast cancer in mammography screenings with greater accuracy than human radiologists.

Drug Discovery and Development: Machine learning algorithms can predict how different chemical compounds will behave and how likely they are to make an effective drug, significantly speeding up the drug discovery process. Atomwise uses AI to analyze the structure of small molecules for drug discovery, reducing the time and costs associated with traditional methods.

FINANCE

Fraud Detection: Machine learning models are adept at identifying patterns indicative of fraudulent transactions. By analysing millions of transactions, these models can detect anomalies that signal fraud, helping financial institutions to minimize losses. Visa uses AI and ML to analyze transaction data in real-time, preventing billions of dollars in fraud annually.

Algorithmic Trading: ML algorithms can analyze market data to make predictive trading decisions faster than human traders. These algorithms can identify trends and patterns in market data, enabling traders and institutions to execute trades at optimal times.

RETAIL AND E-COMMERCE

Personalized Recommendations: Machine learning powers recommendation systems that personalize the shopping experience for users. By analysing past purchase history, browsing behaviour, and preferences, ML models can suggest products that users are more likely to buy. Amazon and Netflix are famous examples, using recommendation engines to suggest products and movies to users.

Inventory Management: AI and ML algorithms optimize inventory levels by predicting demand for products, considering factors like seasonality, trends, and historical sales data. This helps retailers reduce stockouts and overstock, improving profitability.

TRANSPORTATION AND LOGISTICS

Autonomous Vehicles: Deep learning is a key technology behind the development of self-driving cars. These vehicles use deep neural networks to process data from sensors and cameras for object detection, navigation, and decision-making. Companies like Tesla and Waymo are at the forefront, integrating deep learning into their autonomous driving systems.

Supply Chain Optimization: Machine learning models predict supply chain disruptions and optimize routes and inventory levels. UPS uses its ORION (On-Road Integrated Optimization and Navigation) system, which leverages ML to optimize delivery routes, saving millions of miles and gallons of fuel each year.

ENTERTAINMENT AND MEDIA

Content Creation: Deep learning models are now capable of generating realistic images, videos, and text. GPT-3, developed by OpenAI, can produce human-like text, enabling applications from automated news writing to content creation for social media.

Music and Art Generation: AI algorithms can create music and art by learning from vast datasets of existing works. Google's Magenta project explores the role of AI in the creative process, producing songs, drawings, and more.

CONCLUSION

Machine learning and deep learning are not just academic concepts but practical technologies with widespread applications across industries. They are driving efficiency, enabling innovation, and creating new opportunities and business models. As these technologies continue to evolve, their impact on industries and everyday life is expected to grow, heralding a new era of AI-driven transformation.

NEURAL NETWORKS

Neural networks, a foundational element of deep learning and artificial intelligence, are computational models designed to process information in a manner reminiscent of the human brain's architecture. Their development was inspired by our understanding of biological neural networks, where neurons interconnected by synapses process and transmit information through electrical and chemical signals. This section delves into the essence of neural networks, their inspiration from the human brain, and their method of processing information.

INSPIRATION FROM THE HUMAN BRAIN

The human brain is an incredibly complex organ, consisting of approximately 86 billion neurons. These neurons communicate with each other through synapses, forming a vast and intricate network that processes information from our senses, enables thought, memory, and emotions, and controls our actions. Early researchers in artificial intelligence saw the potential to mimic this biological system to create machines capable of learning and making decisions.

Neural networks in AI are simplified models of this biological complexity. They consist of artificial neurons or nodes, which are connected by edges representing synapses. These connections can transmit signals between neurons, and the strength of these signals can be adjusted, which is akin to learning in the human brain.

STRUCTURE OF NEURAL NETWORKS

A typical neural network comprises three types of layers: the input layer, hidden layers, and the output layer.

Input Layer: This layer receives the raw data. Each neuron in the input layer represents a feature of the data being processed. For example, in image recognition, each neuron might correspond to the intensity of a pixel in the image.

Hidden Layers: These layers, potentially multiple in a deep neural network, transform the inputs into something that the output layer can use. As data passes through the hidden layers, the network identifies patterns and features.

The complexity and abstraction of the patterns recognized increase with each subsequent layer, allowing the network to understand complex data.

Output Layer: The final layer produces the network's prediction or decision based on the processed information from the hidden layers.

PROCESSING INFORMATION

The process of information flow in a neural network involves several key steps:

1. Forward Propagation: Data is fed into the input layer, and each input neuron sends it to the neurons in the first hidden layer. The data is transformed at each neuron based on a set of weights (which represent the strength of the connections) and a bias term, followed by the application of an activation function that determines whether and to what extent the signal should progress further through the network.

2. Activation Functions: These functions are crucial as they introduce non-linearity into the network, allowing it to learn and model complex relationships. Without non-linearity, the network would be unable to learn from data that isn't linearly separable.

3. Weight Adjustment: The heart of learning in a neural network lies in adjusting the weights of the connections based on the error of the network's output. This adjustment is typically performed using a technique called backpropagation, where the error is calculated at the output and distributed back through the network, allowing the weights to be updated in a way that minimizes the error.

4. Iteration: This process is repeated across many iterations, with the network continuously adjusting its weights and biases to minimize the difference between its predictions and the actual outcomes. Over time, the network learns to make accurate predictions or decisions based on the input data.

CONCLUSION

Neural networks are a powerful tool in AI, capable of learning from data in a way that mimics the human brain's processing capabilities. By adjusting the connections between artificial neurons, neural networks can learn complex patterns and relationships within data, enabling a wide range of applications from image and speech recognition to natural language processing and beyond. Their ability to learn and improve over time makes them a cornerstone of modern AI and deep learning technologies.

ARCHITECTURE OF NEURAL NETWORKS

Imagine you're trying to teach a robot how to recognize whether a photo contains a cat. This task, which seems simple to humans, requires the robot to learn from numerous examples what features make up a "cat" in an image. This learning process is where neural networks, a key concept in artificial intelligence (AI), come into play. Let's break down the architecture of neural networks into digestible parts: neurons, layers, and activation functions, to understand how they enable a machine to learn from data.

NEURONS: THE BUILDING BLOCKS

Think of neurons in a neural network as tiny detectives, each specializing in recognizing specific types of clues. In our cat photo example, one neuron might focus on identifying edges in the image, another might look for patterns like fur textures, and yet another might concentrate on colours typical of cats.

A neuron receives input (clues) from the data, processes it, and passes on its findings (output) to other neurons. The input to a neuron can come directly from the data (e.g., the pixels of an image) or from the outputs of other neurons. This process is somewhat similar to passing a message along a chain, where each person adds some information based on their expertise.

LAYERS: ORGANIZING THE DETECTIVES

Neural networks are organized into layers, which are essentially teams of neurons working together. There are three main types of layers:

1. Input Layer: This is where the whole investigation begins. The input layer receives the raw data. In our example, this layer's neurons receive the pixel values of the image.

2. Hidden Layers: These are the layers between the input and output layers. You can think of each hidden layer as a team of detectives specializing in different aspects of the investigation. The first hidden layer might identify basic patterns like edges and colours, while subsequent layers might recognize more complex features like shapes and textures. The "depth" of deep learning comes from having multiple hidden layers, each building on the work of the previous one to gradually abstract and refine the understanding of the data.

3. Output Layer: This is where the final decision is made, based on the accumulated evidence from the hidden layers. For our cat-detecting robot, the output layer would conclude whether the image contains a cat.

Activation functions are like the decision-making process each detective (neuron) uses to determine how important the clue they've found is. These functions decide whether the information a neuron has gathered is relevant enough to be passed along to the next layer.

An activation function takes the input processed by a neuron—considering both the evidence (input data) and the neuron's own bias (a value that adjusts the threshold for activation)—and produces an output. If the evidence is strong enough (i.e., the input value is high enough after considering the neuron's bias), the activation function "activates" the neuron, sending its findings to the next layer. Common activation functions include:

ReLU (Rectified Linear Unit): This function outputs the input directly if it is positive; otherwise, it outputs zero. It's like saying, "If the clue is relevant, pass it on; if not, stay quiet."

Sigmoid: This function outputs a value between 0 and 1, effectively squashing the input into this range. It's useful for cases where you need to interpret the output as a probability or when the decision is binary (yes/no).

PUTTING IT ALL TOGETHER

When you feed an image into the neural network, it flows from the input layer through the hidden layers, with each neuron adding its piece of insight, until it reaches the output layer, which makes the final call on whether the image contains a cat.

The beauty of neural networks lies in their ability to learn. By adjusting the connections (weights) between neurons based on feedback (how correct or incorrect the output is), the network gets better over time at making accurate predictions or decisions.

In essence, neural networks mimic the process of learning from experience, refining their detective skills (parameters) with each new piece of evidence (data) they encounter, making them a powerful tool for solving complex, real-world problems in AI.

ADVANCEMENTS ENABLED BY NEURAL NETWORKS

Neural networks, with their intricate architecture inspired by the human brain, have catalysed a revolution in artificial intelligence (AI) and machine learning. These computational models have unlocked unprecedented capabilities in pattern recognition, predictive analytics, and autonomous decision-making, transforming industries and everyday life. Let's explore some of the significant advancements enabled by neural networks.

ENHANCED PATTERN RECOGNITION

Neural networks excel at identifying patterns in vast and complex datasets, a task that is often challenging for traditional computational approaches. This capability is particularly transformative in fields like image and speech recognition:

Image Recognition: Neural networks, especially Convolutional Neural Networks (CNNs), have become adept at analysing visual data. They can identify objects, faces, and even emotions in images and videos with remarkable accuracy. This technology underpins the facial recognition systems used in security and personal devices and enables medical imaging software to detect diseases such as cancer more reliably than ever before.

Speech Recognition: Neural networks have significantly improved the ability of machines to understand and transcribe human speech. This advancement is evident in virtual assistants like Siri, Alexa, and Google Assistant, which can comprehend spoken commands and questions in various languages and accents, making technology more accessible and interactive.

PREDICTIVE ANALYTICS AND DECISION MAKING

The predictive power of neural networks has had a profound impact on industries ranging from finance to healthcare, enabling more informed decision-making based on data-driven insights:

Financial Forecasting: In finance, neural networks are used to predict stock market trends, assess credit risk, and detect fraudulent transactions. By analysing historical data, these models can identify patterns that precede rises or falls in stock prices or flag transactions that deviate from normal behaviour, helping investors and institutions make better decisions.

Healthcare Prognostics: Neural networks analyze patient data to predict disease progression and treatment outcomes. For example, models can forecast the likelihood of patients developing certain conditions, allowing for earlier intervention and personalized treatment plans, thereby improving patient care and outcomes.

AUTONOMOUS SYSTEMS AND ROBOTICS

Neural networks are at the heart of the development of autonomous systems and robotics, enabling machines to navigate and interact with their environments in sophisticated ways:

Self-driving Cars: Neural networks process data from sensors and cameras in real-time to enable autonomous vehicles to recognize objects, predict the behaviour of other road users, and make split-second driving decisions. This technology promises to make transportation safer and more efficient.

Robotic Process Automation (RPA): In manufacturing and logistics, neural networks empower robots to perform complex tasks such as assembling products, picking and packing orders, and even navigating warehouses autonomously, increasing efficiency and reducing the need for human intervention in dangerous or repetitive tasks.

NATURAL LANGUAGE PROCESSING (NLP)

Advancements in NLP, largely driven by neural networks, have enabled machines to understand, interpret, and generate human language with a level of sophistication previously unattainable:

Machine Translation: Neural networks have dramatically improved the quality of machine translation services, breaking down language barriers and facilitating global communication.

Sentiment Analysis: Businesses use neural networks to analyze customer feedback, social media conversations, and reviews to gauge public sentiment toward products, services, or brands, allowing for more responsive and tailored marketing strategies.

CONCLUSION

The advancements enabled by neural networks represent a leap forward in our ability to harness data for insights, automation, and innovation. By recognizing patterns, making accurate predictions, and enabling autonomous decision-making, neural networks are not just solving complex problems but are also opening new frontiers in AI and machine learning. As research and development continue, we can expect neural networks to drive further breakthroughs, reshaping our future in ways we are only beginning to imagine.

FROM DATA TO DECISIONS

Training artificial intelligence (AI) models is a meticulous process that transforms raw data into a decision-making engine. This journey involves several stages, each critical to developing a model that is accurate, reliable, and capable of generalizing its learning to new, unseen data. Central to this process are three types of data sets: training data, validation data, and test data. Let's explore how these data sets are used in the training process and their roles in shaping AI models.

TRAINING DATA: THE FOUNDATION OF LEARNING

Training data is the cornerstone of the AI model training process. It consists of a large set of examples used to teach the model about the specific task it needs to perform, whether it's recognizing objects in images, understanding spoken words, or predicting future trends based on historical data. Each example in the training dataset includes input data (features) and the corresponding output (label), providing the model with patterns to learn from.

Role: The primary role of training data is to expose the model to a wide variety of scenarios and outcomes, allowing it to adjust its internal parameters (such as weights in neural networks) to make accurate predictions or decisions based on the input features.

VALIDATION DATA: TUNING AND VALIDATION

Validation data is a separate dataset not seen by the model during the initial training phase. It is used to evaluate the model's performance and to fine-tune the model's hyperparameters (settings that govern the model's learning process, such as learning rate or the complexity of the model).

Role: The key role of validation data is to provide a reliable metric for how well the model is learning and generalizing from the training data. It helps in identifying issues like overfitting, where the model performs well on the training data but poorly on new, unseen data. By adjusting hyperparameters based on the model's performance on the validation set, developers can improve the model's ability to generalize.

TEST DATA: THE FINAL EXAMINATION

Test data is another set of examples that the model has never seen during training or validation. It is used to evaluate the final model's performance after the training and validation phases are complete. This dataset provides an unbiased assessment of how well the model is expected to perform in the real world.

Role: The test data serves as the final examination for the AI model, testing its ability to apply what it has learned to new data. The performance on the test set gives developers and researchers a clear picture of the model's effectiveness and its potential real-world applicability and limitations.

THE TRAINING PROCESS: AN OVERVIEW

1. Initial Training: The model is trained on the training data, learning to make predictions or decisions based on the input features.

2. Validation and Tuning: The model's performance is evaluated on the validation data, and adjustments are made to the hyperparameters to improve learning and generalization.

3. Final Evaluation: Once the model is fully trained and validated, it is tested on the test data to assess its performance. This step confirms the model's ability to handle new, unseen data.

4. Iteration: Often, the training process is iterative. Based on the performance on the test data, the model might be further refined, additional data might be collected, or the model architecture might be adjusted. This cycle continues until the model achieves the desired level of performance.

CONCLUSION

Training AI models is a complex process that relies heavily on the quality and diversity of the training, validation, and test data. Each type of data plays a unique role in ensuring that the model not only learns effectively from past examples but also generalizes this learning to make accurate predictions about new, unseen data. This careful orchestration of data and learning processes is what enables AI models to make informed decisions, driving advancements across various fields and applications.

KEY CONCEPTS OF AI MODEL TRAINING

Training AI models is a delicate balancing act, where the goal is to achieve a model that accurately predicts or makes decisions based on new, unseen data. This process involves navigating through potential pitfalls such as overfitting and underfitting, while aiming for the sweet spot of generalization. Let's delve into these key concepts to understand their significance in AI model training.

OVERFITTING: THE MEMORIZER

Imagine a student who memorizes facts for an exam without understanding the concepts. While they might perform well on questions identical to their study material, they'll struggle with any question that's even slightly different. This scenario mirrors overfitting in AI model training.

What is Overfitting? Overfitting occurs when an AI model learns the training data too well, capturing noise and random fluctuations along with the underlying patterns. The model becomes excellent at predicting or classifying the training data but performs poorly on new, unseen data because it has essentially memorized the training set rather than learning the general principles.

Signs and Solutions: Overfitting is often detected by a significant discrepancy between the model's performance on the training data versus the validation/test data. Solutions include simplifying the model (reducing its complexity), using regularization techniques (which add constraints to the model to discourage complex co-adaptations on training data), and increasing the amount of training data to cover a broader set of scenarios.

UNDERFITTING: THE UNDERACHIEVER

Conversely, underfitting is like a student who hasn't studied enough: they understand only the most basic concepts and fail to grasp the details necessary for a good exam performance. In AI, underfitting describes a model that hasn't learned enough from the training data.

What is Underfitting? Underfitting occurs when a model is too simple to capture the underlying structure of the data. It can't even perform well on the training data, let alone generalize to new data. This usually happens when the model doesn't have enough capacity (e.g., not enough layers or neurons in a neural network) or the training process was inadequate.

Signs and Solutions: Underfitting is indicated by poor performance on both the training and validation/test datasets. Solutions include increasing the model's complexity, extending the training duration, or improving the feature selection process to ensure the model has enough information and capacity to learn effectively.

GENERALIZATION: THE IDEAL LEARNER

The ultimate goal of training an AI model is generalization - the model's ability to apply what it has learned from the training data to new, unseen data. A well-generalized model is like a student who has understood the course material thoroughly and can apply their knowledge to solve new problems.

Achieving Generalization: Generalization is achieved by finding the right balance between a model's complexity and its training. It requires a model complex enough to capture the key patterns in the data, but not so complex that it starts to memorize the noise. Techniques such as cross-validation (where the training data is divided into subsets to validate the model multiple times), regularization, and using diverse datasets can help in achieving good generalization.

CONCLUSION

Overfitting, underfitting, and generalization are critical concepts in AI model training, representing common challenges that practitioners must navigate. The art of training AI models lies in balancing these aspects to create models that not only perform well on training data but can also adapt their learned knowledge to tackle new, unseen data effectively. Achieving this balance ensures that AI models are robust, reliable, and ready for real-world applications.

CHALLENGES AND STRATEGIES IN TRAINING AI MODELS

Training AI models is a complex process fraught with challenges, from the need for vast datasets to substantial computational resources. However, the field of AI has developed a variety of strategies to address these issues, enhancing model performance and efficiency. Let's explore some of the key challenges and corresponding strategies in training AI models.

Challenge: AI models, especially deep learning models, require large amounts of data to learn effectively. The data must be diverse and representative of the real-world scenarios the model will encounter. Acquiring such datasets can be difficult, expensive, and time-consuming.

Strategies:
Data Augmentation: This involves artificially increasing the size of the dataset by making minor alterations to existing data points (e.g., flipping or rotating images) to generate new data points.

Transfer Learning: Transfer learning allows a model trained on one task to be repurposed on a second related task. For example, a model trained on a large generic image dataset can be fine-tuned with a smaller dataset for a specific task, like identifying specific types of animals.

Synthetic Data Generation: AI can create new, synthetic data that mimics real-world data, providing additional training material for models.

COMPUTATIONAL RESOURCES

Challenge: Training sophisticated AI models requires significant computational power, often necessitating specialized hardware like GPUs (Graphics Processing Units) or TPUs (Tensor Processing Units). This can be prohibitively expensive and limit accessibility for researchers and small organizations.

Strategies:
Cloud Computing: Cloud platforms offer access to high-performance computing resources on-demand, allowing for scalable AI model training without the need for upfront investment in hardware.

Model Pruning: This technique reduces the size of a model by removing unnecessary parameters, which can decrease computational requirements without significantly affecting performance.

Efficient Model Architectures: Developing and using more efficient model architectures that require less computational power for training and inference. Examples include MobileNets and EfficientNets designed for mobile and edge devices.

Challenge: Ensuring that AI models perform well, generalize to new data, and do not succumb to overfitting or underfitting is a continual challenge.

Strategies:
Regularization Techniques: Techniques like L1 and L2 regularization add a penalty on model complexity, discouraging overly complex models that could overfit the training data.

Hyperparameter Tuning: Using methods like grid search, random search, or Bayesian optimization to find the optimal set of hyperparameters that result in the best model performance.

Ensemble Methods: Combining the predictions from multiple models to improve accuracy and robustness. Techniques include bagging, boosting, and stacking.

ETHICAL AND BIAS CONSIDERATIONS

Challenge: AI models can inadvertently learn and perpetuate biases present in their training data, leading to unfair or unethical outcomes.

Strategies:
Bias Detection and Mitigation: Implementing tools and processes to detect and mitigate biases in datasets and model predictions. This includes diversifying training data and applying fairness-aware modelling techniques.

Ethical AI Frameworks: Developing and adhering to ethical guidelines and frameworks that ensure AI models are developed and used responsibly.

CONCLUSION

Training AI models is an intricate process that navigates through a landscape of challenges, from data and computational demands to ethical considerations. The strategies developed to address these challenges are as diverse as the challenges themselves, reflecting the dynamic and innovative nature of the AI field. As AI technology continues to evolve, so too will the approaches to training, ensuring models are not only powerful and efficient but also equitable and accessible.

CHAPTER 3: MACHINE LEARNING IN DEPTH

SUPERVISED VS. UNSUPERVISED LEARNING

Imagine teaching a child to distinguish between cats and dogs. You'd show them pictures of each, clearly saying, "This is a cat" and "This is a dog," until they get the hang of it. This process is quite similar to supervised learning in the world of AI. On the other hand, if you gave the child a mixed box of toy animals without any labels and asked them to group similar ones together, they're engaging in a process akin to unsupervised learning. Let's dive deeper into these intriguing concepts.

SUPERVISED LEARNING: LEARNING WITH LABELS

In supervised learning, our data comes with labels. Just like teaching a child with labelled pictures, we feed the AI system a lot of examples that are already tagged with the correct answer. Each piece of data says, "Here's the input, and here's what you should output." This method is used for:

Classification tasks: Where the output is a category, like spam or not spam in an email filtering system.

Regression tasks: Where the output is a continuous value, like predicting the price of a house based on its features.

The goal of supervised learning is to learn a mapping from inputs to outputs, using the labelled examples, so that when the AI encounters new, unseen inputs, it can accurately predict the corresponding output.

UNSUPERVISED LEARNING: FINDING HIDDEN PATTERNS

Unsupervised learning, on the other hand, deals with data that doesn't have labels. The AI system is given data and must make sense of it on its own, finding patterns and structures without any explicit instructions on what to look for. It's like our child sorting toy animals into groups of similar ones without being told any categories upfront. Unsupervised learning is primarily used for:

Clustering: Grouping data points into clusters of similar items, like segmenting customers based on purchasing behaviour.

Dimensionality Reduction: Simplifying data without losing its essence, which can help in visualizing complex datasets or preparing data for other machine learning tasks.

The aim here is to uncover underlying patterns or distributions in the data that can provide insights or help in further processing.

THE DANCE OF DATA

Imagine supervised learning as a guided dance lesson where the steps are clearly taught, and the goal is to learn a specific routine. Unsupervised learning, then, is like improvisational dance, where the dancer explores movements and patterns on their own to create something new and unexpected.

Both supervised and unsupervised learning have their unique challenges and applications. Supervised learning can achieve high accuracy on tasks with clear objectives and ample labelled data. However, labelling large datasets can be costly and time-consuming. Unsupervised learning, while freeing us from the need for labelled data, often requires more sophistication in interpreting the results and understanding the patterns it uncovers.

CONCLUSION

In the grand scheme of AI, supervised and unsupervised learning are two sides of the same coin, offering different paths to understanding the world through data. Whether we're teaching machines to recognize specific outcomes or to discover the hidden structures within data, these learning paradigms open the door to endless possibilities for innovation and insight. As we continue our journey into machine learning, remember: whether supervised or unsupervised, each learning process brings us closer to creating AI that can truly augment human capabilities.

REAL-WORLD APPLICATIONS OF SUPERVISED LEARNING

Supervised learning, with its foundation in labelled data, powers many of the technologies we use daily, often without even realizing it. By training models on datasets where the correct output is known, supervised learning enables machines to predict outcomes for new, unseen data. Let's explore how this concept is applied in two common real-world applications: spam detection in emails and image recognition.

SPAM DETECTION IN EMAILS

One of the earliest and most relatable applications of supervised learning is spam detection in email services. Here's how it works:

Training Data: The model is trained on a dataset of emails that are already labelled as "spam" or "not spam." Each email in the training set acts as an example from which the model can learn. The features might include specific words or phrases commonly found in spam, the frequency of certain types of punctuation, or the sender's reputation.

Learning Process: The supervised learning algorithm analyses the training data, learning patterns and rules that differentiate spam from legitimate emails. For instance, it might notice that emails containing the words "prize" or "free" in conjunction with a request for personal information are often marked as spam.

Prediction: Once trained, the model can then examine new emails and predict whether they are spam based on the patterns it has learned. When you receive an email, the model processes its content and, based on its learning, assigns it to the spam or inbox folder.

This application of supervised learning helps keep our inboxes clean and saves us from the hassle of manually sorting through potentially harmful or irrelevant messages.

IMAGE RECOGNITION

Image recognition, powered by supervised learning, has seen tremendous advancements in recent years, enabling applications from photo tagging on social media to medical imaging diagnostics. Here's a closer look:

Training Data: The model is trained on a vast dataset of images that are labelled according to their content. For example, images might be tagged with labels like "cat," "dog," or "car." Each label corresponds to the main subject of the image, serving as the correct output for the model to learn from.

Learning Process: During training, the model learns to associate specific patterns in the pixel data with the corresponding labels. It might learn, for instance, that images labelled "cat" often contain two pointy ears, whiskers, and eyes with a particular shape.

Prediction: After training, the model can classify new, unlabelled images based on the features it has learned. When presented with a new image, it analyses the patterns in the pixels and predicts the most likely label for the image, effectively recognizing its content.

In applications like medical imaging, this ability to recognize patterns can assist doctors in diagnosing diseases by identifying signs of conditions such as tumours or fractures in X-rays and MRIs, often with greater accuracy or speed than human practitioners alone.

CONCLUSION

Supervised learning transforms labelled data into models capable of making accurate predictions, from filtering spam in our emails to recognizing the content of images. These applications are just the tip of the iceberg, as supervised learning continues to drive innovation across various fields, making our interaction with technology smoother, safer, and more intuitive.

UNSUPERVISED LEARNING: EXPLORING THE UNLABELED WORLD

Unsupervised learning, a fascinating branch of machine learning, dives into the world of unlabelled data. Unlike its supervised counterpart, unsupervised learning algorithms seek to identify inherent structures, patterns, and relationships within datasets that haven't been explicitly labelled or categorized. This exploration is crucial in scenarios where the data lacks specific outcomes or when the potential insights are unknown. Let's delve into two significant applications of unsupervised learning: customer segmentation and anomaly detection, to understand how these models bring clarity to the chaos of unlabelled data.

CUSTOMER SEGMENTATION

In the realm of marketing and sales, understanding your customer base is paramount. Customer segmentation involves dividing a company's customers into groups that reflect similarity among customers in each group. The goal is to tailor marketing strategies to each segment's unique characteristics and preferences, enhancing customer satisfaction and loyalty.

How Unsupervised Learning Works Here: Unsupervised learning models, particularly clustering algorithms like K-means, hierarchical clustering, and DBSCAN, analyze customer data based on purchasing behaviour, demographics, engagement levels, and preferences. These models identify patterns and relationships within the data, grouping customers into segments based on similarities in their features.

Application Insights: For instance, an e-commerce company might use unsupervised learning to segment its customers into groups such as "frequent high spenders," "occasional bargain hunters," or "loyalty program enthusiasts."

This segmentation allows for targeted marketing campaigns, personalized recommendations, and tailored customer experiences, ultimately driving sales and enhancing customer engagement.

ANOMALY DETECTION

Anomaly detection, also known as outlier detection, is crucial in fields ranging from fraud detection in banking and finance to fault detection in manufacturing processes. It involves identifying rare items, events, or observations which raise suspicions by differing significantly from the majority of the data.

How Unsupervised Learning Works Here: Unsupervised learning models are trained on datasets without any indication of what constitutes normality or anomaly. These models learn the normal distribution of data and can then identify instances that deviate significantly from this norm. Techniques used include isolation forests, one-class SVMs, and autoencoders.

Application Insights: In fraud detection, for example, an unsupervised model can analyze transactions across various features—such as amount, location, and time—to learn typical transaction patterns. It can then flag transactions that deviate from these patterns, indicating potential fraud. Similarly, in manufacturing, unsupervised learning can monitor equipment data to detect anomalies that suggest a malfunction or impending failure, enabling preventive maintenance.

THE POWER OF UNSUPERVISED LEARNING

Unsupervised learning models thrive on the challenge of uncovering hidden structures in unlabelled data, providing valuable insights without the need for predefined categories or labels. In customer segmentation, these models help businesses understand their clientele's diverse needs and preferences, enabling personalized engagement strategies. In anomaly detection, they serve as vigilant guardians, identifying potential issues before they escalate into significant problems.

CONCLUSION

The applications of unsupervised learning in customer segmentation and anomaly detection showcase its ability to find patterns and relationships in unlabelled data, offering a lens through which businesses and organizations can gain insights, enhance operations, and pre-emptively address issues. As unsupervised learning continues to evolve, its potential to unlock new understandings and opportunities across various domains remains vast and largely untapped, promising exciting developments in the exploration of data's hidden layers.

CHALLENGES AND LIMITATIONS OF SUPERVISED LEARNING

Both supervised and unsupervised learning are powerful tools in the machine learning arsenal, each with its unique strengths and applications. However, they also come with their own set of challenges and limitations that can affect their effectiveness and efficiency. Understanding these challenges is crucial for selecting the right approach for a given problem and for developing strategies to mitigate potential issues.

DATA LABELING COSTS

One of the most significant challenges in supervised learning is the need for large amounts of labelled data. Labelling data can be extremely time-consuming and costly, especially for tasks requiring expert knowledge, such as diagnosing medical images or annotating complex texts for natural language processing tasks.

Mitigation Strategies: Strategies to address this challenge include using semi-supervised learning, where a small amount of labelled data is combined with a large amount of unlabelled data, and active learning, where the model is trained iteratively, and only the most informative samples are labelled by experts. Transfer learning, where a model trained on one task is adapted for another related task, can also reduce the need for labelled data in the target domain.

OVERFITTING

Supervised learning models, especially those with high complexity, are prone to overfitting, where the model learns the noise in the training data instead of the underlying pattern, leading to poor performance on new, unseen data.

Mitigation Strategies: Regularization techniques, such as L1 and L2 regularization, can help prevent overfitting by penalizing overly complex models. Cross-validation techniques, where the training data is split into several subsets and the model is trained and validated on these subsets, can also help assess the model's ability to generalize to new data.

CHALLENGES AND LIMITATIONS OF UNSUPERVISED LEARNING

COMPLEXITY OF FINDING HIDDEN STRUCTURES

Unsupervised learning aims to discover hidden patterns or structures in data without predefined labels or outcomes. However, the complexity of the data and the lack of clear success criteria can make it challenging to identify meaningful insights or to determine the optimal number of clusters or dimensions.

Mitigation Strategies: Dimensionality reduction techniques, such as principal component analysis (PCA) and t-distributed stochastic neighbour embedding (t-SNE), can help simplify the data and make underlying patterns more apparent. Choosing the right algorithm and parameters based on domain knowledge and iterative experimentation can also improve the chances of finding meaningful structures.

INTERPRETABILITY AND VALIDATION

The results of unsupervised learning can be difficult to interpret, especially when the algorithm uncovers unexpected patterns or when the dimensionality of the data is reduced. Additionally, without predefined labels, validating the results and assessing the model's performance can be challenging.

Mitigation Strategies: Visualization tools can help interpret the results of unsupervised learning by providing intuitive representations of the data and the patterns identified by the model. Incorporating domain expertise is crucial for validating the results and ensuring they are meaningful and actionable. Using external or surrogate measures of success, such as the silhouette score for clustering, can also provide some indication of the model's performance.

CONCLUSION

Both supervised and unsupervised learning have transformed the landscape of AI and machine learning, offering powerful methods for making predictions and uncovering insights from data. However, the challenges and limitations associated with these approaches, from the costs of data labelling to the complexity of finding hidden structures, necessitate careful consideration and strategic planning. By understanding these challenges and employing appropriate mitigation strategies, practitioners can leverage the strengths of supervised and unsupervised learning to achieve their objectives and drive innovation.

LEARNING BY DOING

Reinforcement Learning (RL) stands out in the machine learning landscape for its unique approach to training models, not through direct instruction or pattern recognition from data, but by interaction and feedback from the environment. This learning paradigm draws inspiration from the way humans and animals learn to make decisions, emphasizing the role of trial, error, and discovery. Let's dive into the core components of RL—agent, environment, actions, states, and rewards—and explore how they interact within an RL model.

THE AGENT

The agent is the learner or decision-maker in the RL framework. Think of the agent as a character in a video game, navigating through various challenges. In machine learning terms, the agent is the algorithm that makes decisions based on its observations and learns from the outcomes of its actions.

THE ENVIRONMENT

The environment encompasses everything the agent interacts with and needs to learn from or adapt to. Continuing with the video game analogy, the environment would be the game world itself, with all its obstacles, rewards, and rules. In RL, the environment is typically modelled as a dynamic system that responds to the agent's actions, providing new situations or states for the agent to react to.

ACTIONS

Actions are the set of possible moves or decisions the agent can make. Each action taken by the agent affects the environment, which in turn influences the future decisions of the agent. The choice of action at each step is crucial, as it determines the trajectory of learning and the eventual success of the agent in achieving its goal.

STATES

A state represents the current situation or condition of the environment from the perspective of the agent. It includes all the information necessary for the agent to make a decision. In a game, a state could be the current positions of all players and objects on the screen. The goal of the agent is to learn a policy—a strategy for choosing actions—based on the state it's in, to maximize its cumulative reward over time.

REWARDS

Rewards are immediate feedback given to the agent from the environment following an action. They are the cornerstone of reinforcement learning, guiding the agent toward beneficial behaviours and away from undesirable ones. A reward can be positive (encouraging a behaviour) or negative (discouraging a behaviour), and the agent's objective is to maximize the total reward it receives over time.

INTERACTION WITHIN AN RL MODEL

The interaction between these components in an RL model follows a cyclical process:

1. Observation: The agent observes the current state of the environment.
2. Decision: Based on this observation, the agent selects an action to perform.
3. Action: The agent performs the action, affecting the environment.
4. Feedback: The environment provides feedback in the form of a new state and an associated reward.
5. Learning: The agent updates its policy based on the feedback to improve its decision-making process.

This cycle repeats, with the agent continuously learning from the consequences of its actions, refining its policy to achieve better outcomes.

CONCLUSION

Reinforcement learning introduces a dynamic and interactive approach to machine learning, where an agent learns to make decisions by doing and receiving feedback. This framework, with its components of agent, environment, actions, states, and rewards, offers a powerful method for training algorithms in complex environments where explicit instruction is impractical. From mastering games to driving autonomous vehicles, RL continues to push the boundaries of what machines can learn and achieve through interaction and feedback.

REINFORCEMENT LEARNING (RL)

Reinforcement learning (RL) has been at the heart of some of the most exciting advancements in AI, demonstrating the power of learning through trial and error. Here are two notable examples:

GAME-PLAYING AI: ALPHAGO

AlphaGo, developed by DeepMind, is a prime example of RL's capabilities. It's an AI system designed to play the board game Go, which is known for its deep strategy and complexity. Unlike traditional game-playing algorithms that rely on brute-force search, AlphaGo uses RL to evaluate board positions and determine the most promising moves.

Learning Process: AlphaGo trained by playing thousands of games against itself, starting from random play and gradually improving. It used a combination of supervised learning (from human game records) and reinforcement learning (from games it played against itself) to refine its strategies.

Outcome: AlphaGo famously defeated world champion Lee Sedol in a five-game match in 2016, a landmark achievement demonstrating RL's potential to tackle problems of immense complexity.

ROBOTICS: LEARNING TO NAVIGATE AND MANIPULATE

In robotics, RL is used to teach robots how to navigate complex environments and manipulate objects with precision. Robots learn through interaction with their environment, improving their actions based on trial and error to achieve specific goals, such as moving items from one place to another or navigating obstacles.

Learning Process: A robot arm, for example, might learn to grasp and move objects by trying different approaches, receiving positive rewards for successful grasps and negative rewards for failures. Over time, it develops an efficient strategy for picking up and moving objects.

Outcome: This approach has enabled robots to perform tasks with a level of dexterity and adaptability that was previously difficult to achieve, opening up new possibilities in manufacturing, logistics, and even in-home care.

These examples underscore the versatility and power of reinforcement learning, showcasing its ability to solve complex, real-world problems by mimicking the natural learning process of trial and error.

The reward function in reinforcement learning (RL) is a critical component that guides the learning process by providing feedback to the agent about the quality of its actions. Essentially, it tells the agent what is good and what is bad in the context of the goals it needs to achieve. The design of the reward function significantly influences the behaviour of the RL agent, making it a powerful tool but also a source of challenges.

Behaviour Shaping: The reward function shapes the agent's behaviour by reinforcing actions that lead towards desired outcomes and penalizing those that do not. It acts as a direct signal to the agent about how well it is performing its task.

Goal Specification: In many RL problems, the reward function is the primary means of specifying the goal of the agent. By carefully defining rewards, developers can guide the agent towards complex objectives without explicitly programming how those objectives should be achieved.

Learning Efficiency: A well-designed reward function can make learning more efficient by providing clear and consistent signals that help the agent quickly understand the consequences of its actions, thereby speeding up the learning process.

CHALLENGES IN DESIGNING REWARD SYSTEMS

Despite its importance, designing effective reward functions is not straightforward and comes with several challenges:

Sparse Rewards: In some environments, useful feedback is rare or difficult to define. For example, in a game, the only clear reward might be winning or losing at the end, making it hard for the agent to learn which actions were beneficial. This can lead to slow learning and require techniques like reward shaping or the use of intrinsic rewards to encourage exploration.

Reward Hacking: Agents might find ways to "hack" the reward system by discovering loopholes that yield high rewards but do not align with the intended goals. For instance, in a cleaning robot scenario, the robot might learn to hide dirt under a carpet rather than actually cleaning, if the reward function only considers visible cleanliness.

Unintended Consequences: Designing rewards that encourage only the desired behaviours without unintended side effects is challenging. An agent might learn to perform the task in a way that maximizes rewards but is unsafe, unethical, or undesirable. For example, an RL-based trading algorithm might learn to take excessive risks that could yield high rewards but also expose it to significant losses.

Balancing Short-term vs. Long-term Rewards: Finding the right balance between rewarding immediate actions and those that are beneficial in the long term can be difficult. Too much emphasis on immediate rewards can lead to short-sighted behaviours, while focusing on long-term rewards may make the learning process inefficient and slow.

CONCLUSION

The design of reward functions in reinforcement learning is both an art and a science, requiring careful consideration of the goals, the environment, and the potential behaviours an agent might adopt. Addressing the challenges associated with reward design is crucial for developing RL agents that behave as intended, efficiently learn to perform their tasks, and avoid unintended or undesirable actions. As the field of RL continues to evolve, so too will the strategies for crafting effective and robust reward systems.

ADVANCED TOPICS IN REINFORCEMENT LEARNING (RL)

Advanced topics in reinforcement learning (RL), such as deep reinforcement learning and policy gradient methods, represent significant strides in the field, enabling the solution of more complex decision-making problems than ever before. These approaches have expanded the applicability of RL to domains like autonomous driving, complex game playing, and robotic control, showcasing the potential of RL to tackle tasks that require a high degree of intelligence and adaptability.

DEEP REINFORCEMENT LEARNING

Deep reinforcement learning combines the representation learning capabilities of deep neural networks with the decision-making prowess of reinforcement learning. This synergy allows agents to process high-dimensional sensory inputs and make decisions based on them, which was a challenging task for traditional RL methods.

Significance: Deep reinforcement learning has been pivotal in solving problems that involve complex, high-dimensional state spaces. For example, it's the technology behind AlphaGo's ability to master the game of Go, a game with a state space so vast that it cannot be fully explored with brute-force search methods.

Applications: Beyond games, deep RL has been applied to robotic manipulation tasks, where robots learn to interact with objects in their environment in a nuanced and precise manner. It's also being explored in autonomous vehicle systems, where the agent must navigate complex, dynamic environments safely.

POLICY GRADIENT METHODS

Policy gradient methods are a class of algorithms in reinforcement learning that focus on directly learning the policy—the agent's strategy for selecting actions—by optimizing it with respect to the expected return (cumulative rewards) using gradient ascent. Unlike value-based methods, which first learn the value of actions and then derive a policy, policy gradient methods learn the policy directly.

Significance: Policy gradient methods are particularly useful for dealing with continuous action spaces and situations where the action space is too large or complex to enumerate. They offer a more flexible approach to learning policies, allowing for stochastic policies (where actions are taken according to a probability distribution) that can explore the environment more effectively.

Applications: These methods have found success in domains such as continuous control tasks (e.g., robotic arm control, where the movements need to be smooth and precise) and in training AI for multiplayer online battle arena (MOBA) games, where the decision space is enormous and the optimal actions are not discrete.

CHALLENGES AND CONTRIBUTIONS

While deep reinforcement learning and policy gradient methods have pushed the boundaries of what's possible with AI, they also come with challenges. Deep RL can require significant computational resources and large amounts of interaction with the environment, which may not be feasible in all scenarios. Policy gradient methods, while powerful, can suffer from high variance in their estimates of the gradient, leading to unstable learning.

Despite these challenges, the contributions of these advanced RL techniques to solving complex decision-making problems are undeniable. They have enabled more natural, efficient, and intelligent behaviours in machines, opening up new possibilities for automation and AI across various fields. As research continues, further advancements in these areas are expected to continue driving the field of reinforcement learning forward, making it an even more powerful tool for tackling the complex challenges of tomorrow.

NEURAL NETWORKS AND HOW THEY MIMIC THE HUMAN BRAIN

Neural networks, inspired by the intricate network of neurons in the human brain, are a cornerstone of artificial intelligence and machine learning. They are designed to recognize patterns and solve complex problems by mimicking the way humans think and learn. At the heart of a neural network is its architecture, which comprises layers of interconnected nodes or neurons. Let's break down this architecture into its fundamental components: the input layer, hidden layers, and output layer, and explore the role of neurons in processing information.

BASIC ARCHITECTURE OF NEURAL NETWORKS

INPUT LAYER

The input layer is the gateway through which data enters the neural network. Each neuron in this layer represents a feature of the input data. For example, in an image recognition task, each input neuron might correspond to the intensity of a pixel in the image. The role of the input layer is to receive the data and pass it on to the next layer without any computation, serving as a distribution panel that channels the data into the network.

HIDDEN LAYERS

The hidden layers are where the magic happens. These layers, which can range from one to many in a deep neural network, are responsible for extracting patterns and features from the input data. Each neuron in a hidden layer receives inputs from the neurons in the previous layer, processes these inputs, and passes the result to the next layer. The "hidden" in their name comes from the fact that they are not directly exposed to the input or output.

Neurons' Role: Neurons in the hidden layers apply weights to their inputs and sum them up; this sum is then passed through an activation function. The activation function introduces non-linearity into the model, allowing the network to learn complex patterns. The weights are adjustable parameters, and the process of learning in a neural network involves finding the optimal set of weights that minimizes the difference between the predicted output and the actual output.

OUTPUT LAYER

The output layer is the final layer of the neural network and is responsible for producing the result. The number of neurons in this layer corresponds to the number of output values the network is designed to predict. For instance, in a classification task, each neuron in the output layer might represent a different class, and the network would output a probability distribution over these classes.

Processing Information: The neurons in the output layer collect the processed information from the last hidden layer, apply their weights and activation function, and produce the final output of the network. This output is then used to make predictions or decisions based on the input data.

CONCLUSION

Neural networks, with their layers of interconnected neurons, mimic the human brain's structure and function to process information, learn from data, and make intelligent decisions. The input layer receives data, the hidden layers extract and process features, and the output layer delivers the network's final decision or prediction. This architecture enables neural networks to tackle a wide range of tasks, from image and speech recognition to natural language processing and beyond, making them a powerful tool in the field of artificial intelligence.

INSPIRATION BEHIND NEURAL NETWORKS

Neural networks in artificial intelligence are inspired by the biological neural networks that constitute the human brain. This inspiration stems from the desire to replicate the brain's ability to learn from experience, recognize patterns, and make decisions. By drawing parallels between artificial and biological neurons, we can better understand how neural networks attempt to mimic human cognition, albeit in a simplified manner.

BIOLOGICAL NEURONS

The human brain comprises approximately 86 billion neurons, each a nerve cell that processes and transmits information through electrical and chemical signals. A biological neuron receives signals from other neurons through its dendrites, processes these signals in its cell body, and passes the output along its axon to other neurons or to muscles or glands.

Key components of a biological neuron include:
Dendrites: Branch-like structures that receive signals from other neurons.
Axon: A long, slender projection that transmits signals to other neurons or muscles.
Synapses: Junctions between neurons where signals are transmitted. The strength of the signal transmission can be adjusted, which is fundamental to learning and memory.

ARTIFICIAL NEURONS

An artificial neuron, the basic unit of a neural network in AI, is a simplified model of a biological neuron. It receives input signals (data), processes them, and produces an output signal. The structure of an artificial neuron includes:

Input Weights: Analogous to dendrites, these weights represent the strength of the input signals. In learning, adjusting these weights is akin to strengthening or weakening synapses in the brain.

Summation Function: This combines the weighted inputs, similar to how a neuron's cell body integrates incoming signals.

Activation Function: Serving a role similar to the axon in a biological neuron, the activation function determines whether the neuron "fires" and what signal to pass on, introducing non-linearity into the process.

REPLICATING ASPECTS OF HUMAN COGNITION

Neural networks attempt to replicate aspects of human cognition through their architecture and learning processes. While a single artificial neuron is quite simple compared to a biological neuron, networks of these artificial neurons can learn complex patterns and perform tasks such as recognizing speech, identifying images, and understanding natural language.

Learning from Experience: Just as the human brain strengthens or weakens synaptic connections based on experiences, neural networks adjust the weights of their connections based on the data they process, learning to improve their performance on tasks over time.

Pattern Recognition: The human brain is exceptional at recognizing patterns, a trait neural networks emulate by identifying patterns in data, whether it's distinguishing faces in photos or understanding spoken words.

Decision Making: Neural networks, through their layered structure and the processing of information from input to output, can make decisions based on the patterns they've learned, similar to decision-making processes in the human brain.

CONCLUSION

While artificial neural networks are inspired by the biological neural networks of the human brain, they are vastly simplified models. The complexity, adaptability, and efficiency of the human brain far exceed current AI capabilities. However, by borrowing principles such as learning from experience and pattern recognition, neural networks have made significant strides in replicating aspects of human cognition, opening up new possibilities in AI and machine learning. As our understanding of the brain improves and computational models become more sophisticated, the gap between artificial and biological neural networks may narrow, leading to even more advanced and capable AI systems.

KEY ADVANCEMENTS IN NEURAL NETWORK DESIGN

Neural networks have undergone significant evolution since their inception, leading to breakthroughs in artificial intelligence that have transformed various fields. Key advancements such as deep learning, convolutional neural networks (CNNs), and recurrent neural networks (RNNs) have been instrumental in these transformations. Let's explore these advancements and their impact, particularly on computer vision and natural language processing (NLP).

DEEP LEARNING

Deep learning refers to neural networks with many layers, allowing for the processing of data in complex and abstract ways. This depth enables the model to learn features at multiple levels of abstraction, from simple edge detection in early layers to the recognition of complex objects in later layers.

Impact: Deep learning has significantly advanced the field of AI, enabling achievements like accurate image and speech recognition, sophisticated natural language understanding, and even the creation of art and music. Its ability to handle vast amounts of data and learn features automatically has made it a cornerstone of modern AI applications.

CONVOLUTIONAL NEURAL NETWORKS (CNNS)

CNNs are a specialized type of neural network designed for processing structured grid data such as images. CNNs use convolutional layers that apply filters to the data, capturing spatial hierarchies and patterns such as edges, textures, and shapes.

Impact on Computer Vision: CNNs have revolutionized computer vision, enabling machines to see and interpret the world with remarkable accuracy. They are the backbone of image recognition, object detection, and video analysis technologies, powering applications from autonomous vehicles to medical image diagnosis and security systems.

RECURRENT NEURAL NETWORKS (RNNS)

RNNs are designed to process sequential data, such as time series or text. Unlike traditional neural networks, RNNs have loops allowing information to persist, simulating a form of memory. This structure makes them ideal for tasks where context and order matter.

Impact on Natural Language Processing (NLP): RNNs, and their more advanced variants like Long Short-Term Memory (LSTM) networks, have significantly advanced NLP. They've improved machine translation, text generation, and speech recognition by enabling models to handle the sequential nature of language, considering the context and the sequence in which words appear.

CONCLUSION

The advancements in neural network design, from deep learning to CNNs and RNNs, have propelled AI into a new era. Deep learning has unlocked the potential for models to learn from data in more complex and abstract ways. CNNs have become the foundation of computer vision, transforming how machines interpret visual information. RNNs have revolutionized NLP, allowing for more nuanced understanding and generation of human language. Together, these advancements have not only pushed the boundaries of what machines can learn and do but have also opened up new possibilities for solving some of the most challenging problems in AI. As these technologies continue to evolve, their impact is expected to grow, further integrating AI into everyday life and work.

CHALLENGES AND ETHICAL CONSIDERATIONS IN NEURAL NETWORKS

Developing and deploying neural networks, while offering immense potential for innovation and efficiency, also introduces a range of challenges and ethical considerations. These issues span from technical hurdles to broader societal concerns, including data privacy, model interpretability, and AI bias. Addressing these challenges is crucial for ensuring the responsible and beneficial use of neural networks.

DATA PRIVACY

Challenge: Neural networks often require vast amounts of data to train, which can include sensitive or personal information. Ensuring the privacy and security of this data is paramount, especially in fields like healthcare or finance.

Ethical Considerations: Developers must adhere to data protection regulations, such as GDPR in Europe, and implement robust data anonymization and encryption techniques. There's also a growing discussion around user consent and the ethical use of data, emphasizing the need for transparency about how data is collected, used, and shared.

MODEL INTERPRETABILITY

Challenge: Neural networks, especially deep learning models, are often seen as "black boxes" due to their complex structures and the intricate way they process information. This lack of interpretability can make it difficult to understand how models make decisions, posing challenges in critical applications where trust and accountability are essential.

Ethical Considerations: Efforts are underway to develop techniques for "explainable AI" that can provide insights into the decision-making process of neural networks. Ensuring model interpretability is crucial for building trust, facilitating error correction, and complying with legal standards that require decisions to be explainable and justifiable.

AI BIAS

Challenge: Neural networks learn to make decisions based on the data they are trained on. If this data contains biases, the models can inadvertently perpetuate or even amplify these biases, leading to unfair or discriminatory outcomes. Examples include facial recognition systems that perform poorly on certain demographic groups and hiring algorithms that favour certain types of candidates.

Ethical Considerations: Addressing AI bias involves multiple strategies, including diversifying training datasets, employing fairness-aware algorithms, and conducting thorough testing across diverse groups before deployment. It's also important to involve stakeholders from diverse backgrounds in the development process to identify and mitigate potential biases early on.

CONCLUSION

The development and deployment of neural networks bring to the forefront a range of ethical considerations that must be carefully navigated. Ensuring data privacy, enhancing model interpretability, and addressing AI bias are not just technical challenges but also ethical imperatives. By tackling these issues head-on, the AI community can work towards the responsible use of neural networks that respects individual rights and promotes fairness and transparency. As neural network technologies continue to evolve, so too will the approaches to addressing these ethical challenges, requiring ongoing dialogue, research, and collaboration across the tech industry, academia, and society at large.

CHAPTER 4: AI IN EVERYDAY LIFE

PERSONAL ASSISTANTS: SIRI, ALEXA, AND GOOGLE ASSISTANT

The journey of personal assistants from rudimentary voice-activated commands to today's AI-powered companions encapsulates a remarkable evolution in artificial intelligence and human-computer interaction. This transformation has turned personal assistants into integral parts of our daily lives, capable of understanding context, performing complex tasks, and offering personalized interactions.

THE EARLY DAYS: VOICE-ACTIVATED COMMANDS

The inception of personal assistants can be traced back to simple voice-activated systems that could perform basic tasks like dialling phone numbers or opening applications on command. These early systems operated on limited voice recognition technology, requiring users to speak specific commands in a clear, precise manner. The interaction was largely one-way, with minimal understanding or contextual awareness.

THE RISE OF AI-POWERED ASSISTANTS

The introduction of AI-powered personal assistants such as Siri, Alexa, and Google Assistant marked a significant leap forward. These assistants leveraged advancements in natural language processing (NLP) and machine learning to understand and process natural human speech in a much more flexible and nuanced way. This shift allowed users to interact with their devices more naturally and conversationally, without needing to memorize specific commands.

CONTEXTUAL UNDERSTANDING AND COMPLEX TASKS

Today's personal assistants are not just voice-activated but are context-aware, capable of understanding the user's intent and the context of queries. This contextual understanding enables them to handle complex, multi-step tasks and provide information or perform actions that are relevant to the user's current situation or past preferences. For instance, they can suggest leaving earlier for an appointment if there's heavy traffic or offer to reorder a frequently purchased item without the user specifying the product.

PERSONALIZED INTERACTIONS

AI personal assistants now offer a level of personalization that was previously unattainable. They learn from individual user interactions, preferences, and behaviours, allowing them to tailor responses, suggestions, and services to each user uniquely. This personalization extends to recognizing different voices in a household, providing personalized news updates, calendar reminders, or music recommendations based on who is speaking.

THE FUTURE: TOWARDS MORE EMPATHETIC COMPANIONS

The evolution of personal assistants is steering towards even more sophisticated AI models that can understand and process emotional cues in speech, making interactions more empathetic and human-like. Future advancements may see personal assistants becoming proactive, anticipating needs based on context, past behaviour, and predictive analytics, further blurring the lines between human and machine interaction.

CONCLUSION

The evolution of personal assistants from basic voice-activated systems to today's AI-powered, contextually aware, and personalized companions highlights the rapid advancements in AI and NLP technologies. As these assistants continue to evolve, they promise to become even more integrated into our daily lives, offering unprecedented levels of assistance, personalization, and companionship.

TECHNOLOGY BEHIND PERSONAL ASSISTANTS

The technology behind personal assistants like Siri, Alexa, and Google Assistant is a sophisticated blend of natural language processing (NLP), speech recognition, and machine learning. These components work in harmony to enable personal assistants to understand, interpret, and respond to user queries in a remarkably human-like manner. Let's delve into how each of these technologies contributes to the functionality of personal assistants.

SPEECH RECOGNITION

Speech recognition is the first step in the process, allowing the assistant to convert spoken words into text. This technology uses sophisticated algorithms to analyze the audio signal, identify phonemes (the smallest units of sound in a language), and construct these into words and sentences based on the language's rules.

How It Works: When you speak to a personal assistant, the device captures your voice as an audio waveform. This waveform is then processed to identify distinct phonetic elements and match them with known word patterns to transcribe the speech into text. Advanced models can filter out background noise and understand different accents, making the system more robust and versatile.

NATURAL LANGUAGE PROCESSING (NLP)

Once the speech is converted to text, NLP comes into play. NLP is a field of AI focused on enabling machines to understand and interpret human language. It involves syntax analysis (understanding the structure of sentences), semantic analysis (interpreting the meaning), and context understanding.

Understanding Intent: NLP algorithms analyze the transcribed text to discern the user's intent—what action the user wants the assistant to perform. This involves parsing the sentence structure, recognizing keywords, and understanding the context to accurately interpret the request.

Dialogue Management: NLP also enables the assistant to manage a conversation with the user, remembering the context of the interaction to provide coherent and relevant responses, even in a prolonged exchange.

MACHINE LEARNING

Machine learning underpins the continuous improvement and personalization of personal assistants. By analysing vast amounts of data on user interactions, machine learning algorithms optimize the assistant's responses over time, making them more accurate and personalized.

Adaptive Learning: Machine learning allows personal assistants to learn from each interaction, adapting their behaviour based on what works best. For example, if a user frequently asks for weather updates in a specific location, the assistant learns to prioritize weather information for that location in future queries.

Personalization: Beyond adapting to general user behaviour, machine learning enables personal assistants to tailor their responses to individual users, recognizing patterns in preferences, speech nuances, and even predicting needs based on past interactions.

INTEGRATION OF COMPONENTS

The integration of speech recognition, NLP, and machine learning technologies allows personal assistants to provide a seamless and intuitive user experience. Here's a simplified overview of how these components work together:

1. Speech to Text: The user's spoken input is captured and converted into text using speech recognition.
2. Text Analysis: NLP processes the text to understand the user's intent and context.
3. Response Generation: Based on the analysis, the assistant determines the most appropriate response or action.
4. Learning: Machine learning algorithms use the interaction data to refine the assistant's future responses and actions.

CONCLUSION

The technology behind personal assistants represents a remarkable fusion of AI disciplines, enabling these systems to understand and engage with users in a natural and meaningful way. As advancements in speech recognition, NLP, and machine learning continue, personal assistants will become even more adept at interpreting and responding to the complexities of human language and behaviour.

IMPACT OF PERSONAL ASSISTANTS ON DAILY LIFE

Personal assistants like Siri, Alexa, and Google Assistant have significantly impacted daily life, weaving themselves into the fabric of our routine activities. Their influence ranges from simplifying tasks to managing smart homes and personal schedules, offering a level of convenience that was once the stuff of science fiction. However, this convenience does not come without its challenges, including privacy concerns and the digital divide.

SIMPLIFYING TASKS AND PROVIDING INFORMATION

Personal assistants have made it easier to perform a variety of tasks without the need for physical interaction with a device. Simple voice commands can accomplish tasks like setting alarms, making phone calls, sending messages, or getting weather updates. This hands-free convenience is particularly beneficial when multitasking or for individuals with mobility or visual impairments.

The integration of personal assistants with smart home technology has transformed living spaces into interconnected, automated environments. Through voice commands, users can control lighting, adjust thermostats, monitor security cameras, and manage other smart devices. This level of control not only enhances convenience but also improves home security and energy efficiency.

PERSONAL SCHEDULES AND REMINDERS

Personal assistants help manage daily schedules, set reminders for appointments, and even suggest the best times to leave for meetings based on current traffic conditions. This proactive management helps users stay organized and can reduce the stress associated with keeping track of numerous commitments.

CHALLENGES AND CONSIDERATIONS

PRIVACY CONCERNS

One of the most significant challenges associated with personal assistants is privacy. These devices are always listening for their wake word, raising concerns about eavesdropping and the potential for sensitive information to be recorded and stored. Moreover, the data collected by personal assistants, including personal preferences and behaviour patterns, could be vulnerable to breaches or misuse.

Mitigation Efforts: Companies have implemented features like mute buttons, the ability to review and delete voice recordings, and more transparent privacy policies. However, users must remain vigilant about their privacy settings and the information they share.

THE DIGITAL DIVIDE

The digital divide refers to the gap between individuals who have access to modern information and communication technology and those who do not. Personal assistants, while convenient, require a reliable internet connection and compatible devices, which may not be accessible to everyone, especially in rural or impoverished areas.

Widening Gap: As personal assistants become more integrated into daily life, there's a risk that the digital divide could widen, leaving those without access at a disadvantage in terms of information access, convenience, and even job opportunities.

CONCLUSION

Personal assistants have undeniably made life more convenient, offering a range of services that simplify tasks, enhance productivity, and make our homes smarter and more efficient. However, the widespread adoption of these technologies also brings to light significant challenges, particularly concerning privacy and the digital divide. Addressing these challenges is crucial to ensuring that the benefits of personal assistants can be enjoyed by all, without sacrificing individual privacy or exacerbating social inequalities.

FUTURE TRENDS AND POTENTIAL DEVELOPMENTS

The landscape of personal assistant technology is rapidly evolving, driven by advancements in artificial intelligence, machine learning, and natural language processing. As we look to the future, several trends and potential developments promise to make personal assistants even more integral to our daily lives. These advancements include enhanced personalization, emotional intelligence, and broader integration across various aspects of life.

ENHANCED PERSONALIZATION

Future personal assistants are expected to offer unprecedented levels of personalization, tailoring their responses, suggestions, and actions to the individual preferences and needs of each user. This will be achieved through deeper learning from user interactions, behaviours, and even physiological states.

Predictive Personalization: Advanced machine learning models will enable personal assistants to predict user needs and preferences before they are explicitly stated, offering suggestions for restaurants, entertainment, or products based on past behaviour and contextual cues.

Context-Aware Interactions: Personal assistants will become more adept at understanding the context of user requests, including location, time of day, and even the emotional state, allowing for more nuanced and relevant interactions.

EMOTIONAL INTELLIGENCE

The incorporation of emotional intelligence into personal assistants represents a significant leap forward. By recognizing and responding to the emotional states of users, personal assistants can offer more empathetic and supportive interactions.

Voice and Facial Recognition: Future developments may include the ability to analyze voice tones, facial expressions, and physiological signals to gauge a user's mood and adjust responses accordingly, offering comfort during stressful times or sharing in the user's excitement during happy moments.

Empathetic Responses: With emotional intelligence, personal assistants could provide mental health support, such as offering calming techniques for anxiety or motivational encouragement, further blurring the lines between human and machine interaction.

INTEGRATION INTO MORE ASPECTS OF DAILY LIFE

Personal assistants are set to become even more deeply integrated into various aspects of daily life, from healthcare and education to transportation and entertainment.

Healthcare: Personal assistants could monitor health metrics through wearable devices, remind patients to take their medication, provide first aid instructions, or even offer preliminary diagnoses based on symptoms described by the user.

Education: They might become personalized tutors, adapting learning materials to the student's pace and learning style, answering questions, and providing feedback on assignments.

Transportation: Integration with autonomous vehicles could see personal assistants planning routes, providing real-time traffic updates, and even taking over some aspects of vehicle control.

Entertainment: Future personal assistants could curate entertainment based on mood and preferences, creating personalized playlists, recommending movies, or even generating interactive stories or games.

CHALLENGES AND CONSIDERATIONS

As personal assistant technology advances, considerations around privacy, security, and ethical use become increasingly important. Ensuring that these technologies respect user privacy, offer secure interactions, and are accessible to all segments of society will be crucial. Additionally, as personal assistants become more human-like in their interactions, questions about dependency, loneliness, and the nature of human-machine relationships will need to be addressed.

CONCLUSION

The future of personal assistant technology holds exciting possibilities, with advancements in personalization, emotional intelligence, and integration poised to make these tools more helpful, empathetic, and indispensable. As we navigate these developments, balancing innovation with ethical considerations will ensure that personal assistants continue to enhance our lives in positive and meaningful ways.

RECOMMENDATIONS SYSTEMS: NETFLIX, AMAZON, AND BEYOND

In the digital age, where the volume of information and products available online can be overwhelming, recommendation systems have emerged as essential tools for filtering and presenting content tailored to individual preferences. These systems analyze vast amounts of data to identify patterns, preferences, and behaviours, enabling them to recommend information, products, or services that users are likely to find interesting or useful.

THE ROLE OF RECOMMENDATION SYSTEMS

Recommendation systems serve a dual purpose: enhancing user experience and driving engagement for service providers. By personalizing the content that users encounter, these systems help users navigate through the noise of abundant choices, making it easier to find what they're looking for or discover new interests.

Personalization: At the heart of recommendation systems is the ability to personalize the user experience. Whether it's suggesting movies on Netflix, products on Amazon, or articles on a news site, these systems use data about a user's past behaviour, preferences, and interactions to tailor suggestions.

Data Analysis: Recommendation systems rely on sophisticated data analysis techniques to make their predictions. They sift through data on user interactions, such as viewing histories, purchase records, and search queries, as well as content attributes like genres, product descriptions, and tags. By applying algorithms to this data, they can uncover relationships between users and content and predict what a user might like next.

HOW RECOMMENDATION SYSTEMS WORK

There are several approaches to building recommendation systems, each with its strengths and applications:

Collaborative Filtering: This method makes recommendations based on the collective preferences of many users. If a user A has similar tastes to user B, then the recommendations for user A can include items that user B likes but user A hasn't yet encountered. Collaborative filtering can be further divided into user-based and item-based approaches.

Content-Based Filtering: Unlike collaborative filtering, content-based filtering focuses on the attributes of the items themselves. If a user likes certain items, the system recommends items that are similar in content or features to those the user has shown interest in.

Hybrid Approaches: Many modern recommendation systems combine collaborative filtering, content-based filtering, and other methods to improve accuracy and cover more scenarios. Netflix, for example, uses a hybrid model that incorporates user behaviour, content metadata, and even contextual information to provide personalized recommendations.

THE IMPACT OF RECOMMENDATION SYSTEMS

The influence of recommendation systems extends beyond just convenience for users. They play a crucial role in the business strategies of online platforms, increasing user engagement, satisfaction, and retention. By presenting users with content that aligns with their interests, these systems drive discovery, keep users engaged longer, and can significantly boost sales or viewership.

However, the effectiveness of recommendation systems hinges on their ability to accurately understand user preferences and to present diverse and relevant suggestions. Challenges such as creating echo chambers, where users are only exposed to content that reinforces their existing views, or the risk of over-personalization, limiting discovery, are ongoing areas of research and development.

CONCLUSION

Recommendation systems have become an integral part of the digital experience, guiding users through the vast digital landscape to find content that resonates with their preferences and interests. As technology evolves, so too will the sophistication of these systems, promising even more personalized and engaging online experiences.

ALGORITHMS THAT POWER RECOMMENDATION SYSTEMS

Recommendation systems are the engines behind the personalized suggestions we encounter across various digital platforms, from e-commerce sites like Amazon to streaming services like Netflix. These systems rely on sophisticated algorithms to sift through vast amounts of user data and content information, identifying patterns and preferences to make tailored recommendations. The primary algorithms driving these systems are collaborative filtering, content-based filtering, and hybrid approaches. Let's explore how each of these algorithms works and contributes to the personalization of suggestions.

COLLABORATIVE FILTERING

Collaborative filtering is based on the premise that users who agreed in the past will agree in the future about certain preferences. It makes recommendations based on the collective ratings or interactions of users, leveraging the wisdom of the crowd to suggest items.

User-Based Collaborative Filtering: This approach recommends items by finding similar users. For example, if User A and User B have rated several movies similarly, the system might recommend to User A the movies that User B liked (and A hasn't seen yet). Similarity between users is often calculated using metrics like cosine similarity or Pearson correlation.

Item-Based Collaborative Filtering: Instead of finding similar users, this method finds similar items based on user ratings or interactions. If a user likes a particular item, the system recommends items that other users with similar tastes have liked. This approach tends to be more stable over time than user-based filtering since item preferences change less frequently than user preferences.

CONTENT-BASED FILTERING

Content-based filtering focuses on the attributes of the items themselves, recommending items similar to those a user has liked in the past. It analyses the content of items (such as genres, keywords, and descriptions) and a user's interaction history to make suggestions.

How It Works: If a user frequently watches sci-fi movies, the system might recommend other movies within the sci-fi genre. The algorithm uses item features (e.g., genre tags, descriptions) to build a profile of the user's preferences and then scores unseen items based on their similarity to this profile.

HYBRID APPROACHES

Hybrid approaches combine collaborative filtering, content-based filtering, and sometimes other methods to overcome the limitations inherent in each approach and improve recommendation quality.

Combining Methods: A hybrid system might start with collaborative filtering to find a broad set of recommendations and then refine these suggestions using content-based filtering to better match the user's specific interests. Alternatively, it might use both approaches in parallel and merge the recommendations.

Advantages: Hybrid systems can provide more accurate recommendations, especially in scenarios where data is sparse (the "cold start" problem for new users or items). They can also balance the diversity of recommendations, ensuring users are exposed to a wider range of content.

ANALYZING USER DATA

Regardless of the approach, the core of recommendation systems lies in their ability to analyze and learn from user data. This involves:

Data Collection: Gathering data on user interactions (clicks, views, purchases, ratings) and item attributes (descriptions, tags, categories).

Pattern Recognition: Using machine learning algorithms to identify patterns in the data, such as preferences for certain item features or similarities among users or items.

Prediction and Personalization: Applying the learned patterns to predict user preferences for unseen items and generate personalized recommendations.

CONCLUSION

The algorithms that power recommendation systems—collaborative filtering, content-based filtering, and hybrid approaches—each offer unique advantages in analysing user data and making personalized suggestions. By leveraging these algorithms, recommendation systems can significantly enhance user experience, driving engagement and satisfaction across various digital platforms. As these technologies continue to evolve, we can expect even more sophisticated and nuanced recommendation capabilities.

BENEFITS AND CHALLENGES OF RECOMMENDATION SYSTEMS

Recommendation systems have become ubiquitous in the digital landscape, guiding users through the vast expanse of content available online and helping them discover products and services that match their interests and needs. While these systems offer significant benefits by enhancing user experience and driving engagement, they also present challenges and ethical considerations that need careful navigation.

BENEFITS OF RECOMMENDATION SYSTEMS

ENHANCED USER EXPERIENCE

Recommendation systems personalize the user experience, making it easier for users to find content or products that interest them without extensive searching. This personalization can significantly improve user satisfaction and loyalty, as users feel that the platform understands their preferences and caters to their needs.

DISCOVERY OF NEW PREFERENCES

One of the key strengths of recommendation systems is their ability to introduce users to items they might not have found on their own. By analysing user behaviour and preferences, these systems can suggest products, movies, or articles that are similar but not identical to what users have liked in the past, broadening their horizons and encouraging exploration.

INCREASED ENGAGEMENT AND CONVERSION

For businesses, recommendation systems can drive significant benefits by increasing user engagement and conversion rates. Personalized recommendations keep users engaged with the platform longer, leading to more opportunities for content consumption or purchases. This increased engagement often translates into higher sales and revenue.

CHALLENGES AND ETHICAL CONSIDERATIONS

DATA PRIVACY

The effectiveness of recommendation systems is heavily reliant on collecting and analysing vast amounts of user data. This raises significant privacy concerns, as users may not be fully aware of the extent of data collection or how their information is being used. Ensuring data privacy and securing user consent are paramount to maintaining trust and complying with regulations like GDPR.

THE ECHO CHAMBER EFFECT

Recommendation systems can sometimes create "echo chambers" or "filter bubbles," where users are continually exposed to content that reinforces their existing beliefs and preferences. This can limit exposure to diverse viewpoints and content, potentially leading to polarization and reduced content discovery. Balancing personalized recommendations with the need to introduce diversity and novelty is a complex challenge.

OVER-PERSONALIZATION

While personalization is a key benefit of recommendation systems, over-personalization can lead to a narrow focus, where users are only exposed to a limited range of content. This can hinder the discovery of new interests and reduce the overall user experience. Striking the right balance between personalization and diversity is crucial.

CONCLUSION

Recommendation systems play a critical role in modern digital platforms, offering significant benefits by enhancing user experience and driving business metrics. However, the challenges and ethical considerations they present, including data privacy concerns, the risk of creating echo chambers, and the potential for over-personalization, require careful attention. Addressing these challenges involves a combination of transparent data practices, ethical AI development, and algorithms designed to promote diversity and discovery. As recommendation systems continue to evolve, finding the right balance between personalization and user welfare will be key to their long-term success and acceptance.

ADVANCEMENTS IN AI FOR IMPROVED ACCURACY AND PERSONALIZATION

THE FUTURE OF RECOMMENDATION SYSTEMS

The future of recommendation systems is poised at an exciting juncture, with advancements in artificial intelligence (AI) set to redefine how these systems understand user preferences, enhance personalization, and tackle ethical challenges. As AI technologies evolve, we can anticipate significant improvements in the accuracy and personalization of recommendation systems, along with a greater emphasis on transparency and ethical responsibility.

DEEP LEARNING AND COMPLEX MODELS

Future recommendation systems will likely leverage deeper and more complex neural network architectures that can process vast amounts of data more effectively. These models will be capable of understanding nuances in user behaviour and preferences, leading to highly accurate and personalized recommendations.

NATURAL LANGUAGE PROCESSING (NLP)

Advancements in NLP will enable recommendation systems to better understand user queries, reviews, and feedback in natural language, allowing for more nuanced recommendations. For instance, systems could analyze the sentiment behind user reviews to refine their understanding of preferences.

CONTEXTUAL AND REAL-TIME RECOMMENDATIONS

Emerging AI technologies will facilitate more sophisticated contextual and real-time recommendations. Systems will consider not just historical data but also real-time context, such as current events, weather, or even a user's mood, to make more relevant and timely suggestions.

EVOLVING TOWARDS TRANSPARENCY AND ETHICAL RESPONSIBILITY

EXPLAINABLE AI (XAI)

As recommendation systems become more complex, there will be a growing need for explainable AI that can elucidate how recommendations are generated. This transparency is crucial for building trust with users and for complying with regulatory requirements that demand explanations for automated decisions.

ADDRESSING BIAS AND PROMOTING DIVERSITY

Future recommendation systems will incorporate advanced techniques to detect and mitigate bias in recommendations. This includes algorithms designed to ensure diversity and fairness in the content being recommended, actively counteracting the echo chamber effect and promoting a broader range of content.

PRIVACY-PRESERVING TECHNOLOGIES

Advancements in privacy-preserving technologies, such as federated learning and differential privacy, will enable recommendation systems to learn from user data without compromising individual privacy. These technologies will allow systems to aggregate insights across many users while keeping personal data localized and secure.

INTEGRATING ETHICAL CONSIDERATIONS INTO SYSTEM DESIGN

As recommendation systems continue to evolve, integrating ethical considerations into the design and deployment of these systems will become paramount. This includes:

User Control and Customization: Providing users with more control over the recommendations they receive and the data used to generate them, allowing for a more personalized and consensual experience.

Regulatory Compliance and Standards: Adhering to emerging regulations and standards focused on digital ethics, data protection, and AI governance to ensure that recommendation systems operate within ethical and legal boundaries.

Interdisciplinary Collaboration: Encouraging collaboration between technologists, ethicists, policymakers, and user communities to address the multifaceted challenges posed by recommendation systems and to ensure that they serve the broader interests of society.

CONCLUSION

The future of recommendation systems is marked by the potential for significant advancements in AI that promise to enhance personalization and accuracy while addressing critical ethical challenges. By embracing transparency, ethical responsibility, and user-centric design, recommendation systems can continue to enrich our digital experiences in ways that are both innovative and aligned with societal values.

SMART HOMES AND IOT

The concepts of smart homes and the Internet of Things (IoT) represent a significant shift towards more interconnected and automated living environments. At the core of this transformation is the integration of artificial intelligence (AI), which plays a pivotal role in enhancing the functionality, efficiency, and convenience of these technologies. Let's explore what smart homes and IoT entail and how AI fuels this connected world.

SMART HOMES

A smart home is a residence equipped with a series of devices and appliances that can communicate with one another and be managed remotely through a user interface. This setup allows homeowners to control lighting, climate, entertainment systems, and security devices with ease, either through voice commands, mobile apps, or automation.

AI Integration: In smart homes, AI enhances the user experience by learning from the homeowner's habits and preferences to automate tasks. For example, an AI system can learn to adjust the thermostat based on the time of day or presence of people in the home, ensuring optimal comfort while maximizing energy efficiency.

INTERNET OF THINGS (IOT)

The Internet of Things refers to the network of physical objects ("things") embedded with sensors, software, and other technologies for the purpose of connecting and exchanging data with other devices and systems over the internet. IoT encompasses a wide range of devices, from household appliances to industrial machinery, all designed to collect, share, and act on data.

AI Integration: AI plays a crucial role in the IoT by analysing the vast amounts of data generated by connected devices to make intelligent decisions. For instance, AI can predict when a machine is likely to fail and suggest preventive maintenance, or it can optimize a supply chain by analysing real-time data from various sources.

CREATING INTERCONNECTED AND AUTOMATED ENVIRONMENTS

The synergy between smart homes, IoT, and AI leads to the creation of environments that are not only interconnected but also capable of automation and self-optimization. Here's how AI integrates with these technologies:

Learning and Adaptation: AI systems continuously learn from interactions and data, allowing them to adapt to the users' changing needs and preferences. Over time, these systems can automate routine tasks, such as turning off lights when a room is unoccupied or ordering groceries when supplies run low.

Predictive Analysis: By analysing patterns in data, AI can make predictions that enhance efficiency and convenience. For example, a smart thermostat can predict the homeowner's return and adjust the temperature accordingly, ensuring the home is comfortable upon arrival.

Enhanced Security: AI enhances the security of smart homes and IoT devices by detecting anomalies that could indicate a security breach. It can also automate responses to security threats, such as locking down systems or alerting homeowners.

CHALLENGES AND CONSIDERATIONS

While the integration of AI with smart homes and IoT offers numerous benefits, it also presents challenges, including privacy concerns, the potential for over-reliance on technology, and the need for interoperability among devices from different manufacturers. Addressing these challenges is crucial for realizing the full potential of these interconnected and automated environments.

CONCLUSION

Smart homes and the Internet of Things represent the forefront of creating more connected, efficient, and intelligent living and working environments. The integration of AI is central to this transformation, offering the ability to learn from data, automate tasks, and make predictive decisions. As these technologies continue to evolve, they promise to make our homes and cities smarter, safer, and more sustainable, heralding a new era of convenience and connectivity.

KEY APPLICATIONS OF AI IN SMART HOMES AND IOT

The integration of Artificial Intelligence (AI) into smart homes and the Internet of Things (IoT) has led to the development of highly efficient, responsive, and personalized environments. AI's ability to learn from data and adapt to users' habits and preferences is at the core of several key applications in these domains, including energy management, security, and health monitoring. Let's explore how AI enhances these applications by making them more intuitive and aligned with individual needs.

ENERGY MANAGEMENT

AI significantly contributes to energy management in smart homes by optimizing the use of resources, thereby reducing waste and saving costs.

Learning from User Behaviour: AI systems can learn from users' habits—such as their preferred temperatures, typical at-home hours, and usage patterns of appliances—to optimize heating, cooling, and electricity usage without compromising comfort. For example, a smart thermostat can learn to lower the heating when the house is empty and warm it up right before the occupants usually return.

Predictive Analysis for Efficiency: Beyond reacting to immediate data, AI can predict future needs based on weather forecasts, anticipated energy prices, and the household's historical data. This allows for pre-emptive adjustments to energy consumption, such as pre-cooling the house during off-peak hours on a hot day expected to have high energy demand.

SECURITY

In the realm of security, AI elevates the capabilities of smart home systems and IoT devices to offer more proactive and nuanced protection measures.

Anomaly Detection: AI systems monitor for unusual activity that could indicate a security breach, such as unexpected entry or movements at odd hours. By learning what constitutes normal activity for a household, AI can effectively distinguish between routine events and potential threats.

Facial Recognition and Access Control: Advanced AI algorithms can recognize the faces of family members, friends, and regular visitors to manage access control, sending alerts if an unrecognized person is at the door. This feature combines convenience with enhanced security, allowing for keyless entry for known individuals and alerting homeowners to possible intruders.

HEALTH MONITORING

AI's role in health monitoring within smart homes and through IoT devices is rapidly expanding, offering revolutionary ways to care for individuals, especially the elderly and those with chronic conditions.

Behavioural Patterns and Anomaly Detection: By continuously monitoring health-related data, such as activity levels, sleep patterns, and vital signs, AI can identify deviations from normal patterns that may indicate health issues. For instance, a sudden decrease in activity or disrupted sleep patterns could trigger alerts for further investigation.

Personalized Health Insights and Recommendations: AI can provide personalized health insights and recommendations by analysing data from wearables and other health-monitoring devices. This can include suggestions for more physical activity, reminders to take medication, or prompts to schedule a doctor's visit based on detected health trends.

ADAPTIVE LEARNING AND PERSONALIZATION

Across all these applications, the power of AI lies in its ability to learn from and adapt to individual user habits and preferences. This learning process involves:

Data Collection and Analysis: Continuously gathering data from interactions, sensors, and user inputs to build a comprehensive understanding of user habits, preferences, and needs.

Pattern Recognition: Using machine learning algorithms to identify patterns in the data, enabling the system to make informed predictions and decisions.

Feedback Loops: Incorporating user feedback to refine and adjust the system's behaviour, ensuring that the AI's actions remain aligned with user preferences and needs over time.

CONCLUSION

AI's integration into smart homes and IoT devices is transforming how we manage energy, secure our homes, and monitor health by creating systems that learn from us and adapt to our needs. As AI technologies continue to evolve, we can expect these applications to become even more sophisticated, offering unprecedented levels of personalization and convenience in our daily lives.

CHALLENGES AND CONSIDERATIONS IN CREATING SMART HOMES

The proliferation of smart homes, powered by the Internet of Things (IoT) and Artificial Intelligence (AI), promises enhanced convenience, efficiency, and security. However, the journey towards fully integrated smart homes is fraught with challenges and considerations that must be addressed to realize their full potential. Key among these are issues of interoperability, security vulnerabilities, and the potential for over-reliance on technology.

INTEROPERABILITY

One of the primary challenges in creating smart homes is ensuring interoperability among a diverse array of devices and systems from different manufacturers. Smart homes typically involve a wide range of devices, including thermostats, lighting systems, security cameras, and appliances, each potentially using different standards and protocols for communication.

Standardization Efforts: Efforts are underway to develop and adopt universal standards and protocols that enable seamless communication and integration among devices, regardless of the manufacturer. However, achieving widespread adoption remains a challenge.

User Experience: Lack of interoperability can significantly degrade the user experience, making the management of smart home devices more complex and less intuitive. Users may need to navigate multiple apps or interfaces to control different aspects of their home, diminishing the convenience that smart homes are supposed to offer.

SECURITY VULNERABILITIES

As smart homes rely increasingly on connected devices, they become more susceptible to cybersecurity threats. Each connected device represents a potential entry point for hackers, and the personal nature of home data heightens the risks associated with security breaches.

Data Privacy: Smart home devices collect vast amounts of personal data, including habits, routines, and even conversations. Ensuring the privacy and security of this data is paramount, requiring robust encryption and secure data handling practices.

Ongoing Maintenance: Many smart home devices may not receive regular software updates, leaving known vulnerabilities unpatched. Manufacturers and users must prioritize ongoing maintenance and updates to secure devices against evolving threats.

OVER-RELIANCE ON TECHNOLOGY

The convenience and automation offered by smart homes also raise concerns about over-reliance on technology. As homes become smarter, there's a risk that individuals may become too dependent on technology for everyday tasks, potentially impacting their ability to perform these tasks independently.

Skill Degradation: Over-reliance on smart home technology could lead to a degradation of basic skills, such as cooking or navigating, as individuals grow accustomed to automated assistance.

System Failures: Dependence on smart home technology also raises concerns about what happens when these systems fail, whether due to technical glitches, power outages, or cyberattacks. Users must have contingency plans for managing their homes in the absence of smart technology.

CONCLUSION

Creating smart homes that are secure, interoperable, and enhance rather than diminish our capabilities requires careful consideration and proactive management of the challenges involved. Addressing issues of interoperability and security vulnerabilities is crucial for building trust in smart home technologies and ensuring their sustainable integration into our lives. Moreover, fostering a balanced relationship with technology, where convenience does not lead to over-reliance, is essential for maintaining independence and resilience in an increasingly connected world.

FUTURE POSSIBILITIES FOR SMART HOMES AND IOT ENABLED BY AI

The integration of Artificial Intelligence (AI) with smart homes and the Internet of Things (IoT) is not just transforming how we interact with our living spaces; it's also paving the way for significant societal benefits. From promoting sustainable living to enhancing health and well-being, and addressing the challenges of urbanization and aging populations, AI-enabled smart homes and IoT devices hold immense potential for the future.

AI can optimize energy consumption in smart homes, significantly reducing waste and promoting sustainability. By analysing data from various sensors and devices, AI can manage heating, cooling, lighting, and appliance use more efficiently than ever before.

Energy Efficiency: AI systems can predict energy needs based on weather forecasts, occupancy patterns, and user preferences, adjusting smart thermostats and lighting accordingly to minimize energy use without compromising comfort.

Resource Management: Beyond energy, AI can help manage water usage, waste disposal, and even the integration of renewable energy sources like solar panels into the home, making sustainable living more accessible and automated.

ENHANCED HEALTH AND WELL-BEING

Smart homes equipped with AI and IoT devices can play a crucial role in monitoring health and promoting well-being, offering especially crucial support for elderly or disabled individuals living independently.

Remote Health Monitoring: Wearable devices and embedded sensors can track vital signs, detect falls, and monitor movement, allowing for real-time health monitoring and alerts to caregivers or medical professionals in case of emergencies.

Mental Health and Comfort: AI can also contribute to mental well-being by personalizing the living environment—adjusting lighting, temperature, and even playing music or sounds that reduce stress or improve mood.

ADDRESSING URBANIZATION AND AGING POPULATIONS

As urban populations grow and societies face the challenges of supporting aging populations, AI-enabled smart homes and IoT devices offer solutions to enhance quality of life and independence.

Smart Urban Environments: In densely populated urban areas, AI can help manage infrastructure more efficiently, from optimizing traffic flow to improving public safety and environmental monitoring, creating more liveable and sustainable cities.

Aging in Place: For aging populations, AI-enhanced smart homes can provide the support needed to live independently longer, from reminders to take medication to systems that facilitate easy communication with family, friends, and healthcare providers. This not only improves the quality of life for the elderly but also reduces the strain on healthcare systems.

ETHICAL AND SOCIAL CONSIDERATIONS

As we embrace the potential of AI in smart homes and IoT, it's crucial to consider ethical and social implications, including privacy concerns, data security, and ensuring equitable access to these technologies. Balancing innovation with these considerations is key to realizing the full potential of AI in creating more sustainable, healthy, and inclusive living environments.

CONCLUSION

The future possibilities for smart homes and IoT enabled by AI are vast and varied, offering the potential to significantly impact sustainable living, health and well-being, and the challenges posed by urbanization and aging populations. As technology continues to evolve, the focus will be on harnessing these advancements in a way that maximizes benefits while addressing ethical and social challenges, ensuring that the smart homes of the future enhance the lives of all who inhabit them.

CHAPTER 5: THE POWER OF NATURAL LANGUAGE PROCESSING (NLP)

HOW AI UNDERSTANDS AND GENERATES HUMAN LANGUAGE

FUNDAMENTALS OF NLP

Natural Language Processing (NLP) stands as a cornerstone of AI's interaction with human language, enabling machines to parse, understand, and even generate text that is meaningful to humans. This capability is underpinned by several foundational technologies, including syntax analysis, semantic analysis, and sentiment analysis. Each plays a crucial role in deciphering the complexities of human language, from its grammatical structure to its inherent meanings and emotional undertones.

SYNTAX ANALYSIS

Syntax analysis, or syntactic analysis, involves examining the grammatical structure of language. It helps AI determine how words are organized within sentences, identifying parts of speech (nouns, verbs, adjectives, etc.), and understanding the relationships between them. This process is akin to parsing sentences into their constituent elements, such as subjects, predicates, and objects, to build a "parse tree" that represents the syntactic structure of the sentence.

How It Enables AI Understanding: Syntax analysis allows AI to comprehend the basic structure of language, which is essential for making sense of sentences. By understanding syntax, AI can perform tasks like grammar checking, sentence segmentation, and part-of-speech tagging, which are foundational for more complex NLP applications.

SEMANTIC ANALYSIS

Semantic analysis dives deeper, moving beyond the structure of language to interpret meaning. It involves understanding the meanings of individual words, phrases, and sentences in context. This process is challenging due to the nuances of human language, including ambiguity, idioms, and variations in meaning based on context.

How It Enables AI Understanding: Semantic analysis enables AI to grasp the intended meanings behind words and sentences, allowing for the accurate interpretation of queries and texts. This understanding is crucial for applications like machine translation, question-answering systems, and text summarization, where grasping the meaning is essential for accurate output.

SENTIMENT ANALYSIS

Sentiment analysis, or opinion mining, extends NLP's capabilities to detecting and interpreting emotions and sentiments expressed in text. It involves analysing words and phrases to classify the sentiment of the text as positive, negative, or neutral, often at varying levels of intensity.

How It Enables AI Understanding: Sentiment analysis allows AI to understand the emotional tone behind human language, providing insights into people's opinions, attitudes, and emotions. This capability is particularly valuable in areas like social media monitoring, market research, and customer service, where understanding public sentiment or customer satisfaction is crucial.

INTEGRATION FOR COMPREHENSIVE UNDERSTANDING

The integration of syntax, semantic, and sentiment analysis enables AI to achieve a comprehensive understanding of human language. Syntax analysis lays the groundwork by deciphering the structure of language, semantic analysis builds on this to extract meaning, and sentiment analysis adds a layer of emotional intelligence. Together, these technologies empower AI systems to interact with human language in nuanced and meaningful ways, supporting a wide range of applications that require not just the understanding of words and sentences, but also the context, intent, and emotions they convey.

CONCLUSION

The foundational technologies behind NLP—syntax analysis, semantic analysis, and sentiment analysis—collectively enable AI to navigate the complexities of human language. By understanding the structure, meaning, and emotional tone of language, AI can engage in tasks that range from simple translations to complex interactions that require a deep understanding of human communication. As these technologies continue to evolve, we can expect AI's proficiency in understanding and generating human language to reach new heights, further blurring the lines between human and machine communication.

THE ROLE OF MACHINE LEARNING AND DEEP LEARNING IN NLP

The integration of machine learning and deep learning into Natural Language Processing (NLP) has revolutionized the field, significantly enhancing AI's capabilities in understanding and generating human language. These advancements have been driven by the development of sophisticated neural network architectures, including the transformative impact of models like transformers. Let's explore how these technologies have propelled NLP forward.

MACHINE LEARNING IN NLP

Machine learning, particularly in its application to NLP, has shifted the paradigm from rule-based systems to models that learn language patterns from data. Early machine learning approaches in NLP involved algorithms like decision trees, support vector machines, and linear regression, applied to tasks such as spam detection, sentiment analysis, and topic classification. These methods relied on handcrafted features extracted from text, requiring significant expertise and effort to design.

Advancement: The transition to machine learning allowed for automatic feature learning, where the model identifies useful patterns in the data, reducing the reliance on manual feature engineering and enabling more scalable and flexible NLP solutions.

DEEP LEARNING AND NEURAL NETWORKS

The advent of deep learning marked a further leap in NLP's capabilities. Deep learning uses neural networks with multiple layers (hence "deep") to learn representations of data at multiple levels of abstraction, making it particularly effective for processing the sequential and hierarchical nature of language.

Recurrent Neural Networks (RNNs): RNNs and their variants, such as Long Short-Term Memory (LSTM) networks, were among the first deep learning models to significantly impact NLP. They are designed to handle sequential data, making them suitable for tasks like language modelling and machine translation. However, RNNs can struggle with long sequences due to issues like vanishing gradients.

Convolutional Neural Networks (CNNs): While primarily known for their success in computer vision, CNNs have also been applied to NLP tasks. They excel at extracting spatial hierarchies of features, which can be useful for tasks like sentence classification and sentiment analysis.

TRANSFORMERS AND THE RISE OF ATTENTION MECHANISMS

The introduction of the transformer model represented a ground-breaking development in NLP. Transformers rely on attention mechanisms, which allow the model to weigh the importance of different words in a sentence dynamically, providing a more nuanced understanding of language context.

Self-Attention: Unlike RNNs and CNNs, transformers use self-attention to process all words in a sentence simultaneously, making them highly efficient and effective at capturing long-range dependencies in text.

BERT and GPT: Transformer-based models like BERT (Bidirectional Encoder Representations from Transformers) and GPT (Generative Pre-trained Transformer) have set new standards for a wide range of NLP tasks. BERT excels at understanding context in language by pre-training on a large corpus of text and then fine-tuning for specific tasks. GPT, on the other hand, has demonstrated remarkable language generation capabilities, producing coherent and contextually relevant text based on prompts.

IMPACT ON NLP

The impact of machine learning, deep learning, and specifically transformer models on NLP has been profound:

Enhanced Language Understanding: AI can now understand context, nuance, and even the implied meaning in text, enabling more accurate and sophisticated language processing.

Improved Language Generation: AI-generated text has become more coherent, contextually appropriate, and indistinguishable from human-written text in some applications.

Scalability and Efficiency: Transformer models, despite their complexity, have enabled more efficient training and inference processes, making advanced NLP capabilities more accessible.

CONCLUSION

The integration of machine learning and deep learning, especially through neural networks and transformer models, has significantly advanced NLP. These technologies have not only improved AI's understanding and generation of human language but have also opened new possibilities for applications that require deep linguistic and contextual comprehension. As these models continue to evolve, we can expect further innovations and enhancements in the field of NLP.

CHALLENGES IN NLP

Natural Language Processing (NLP) stands as one of the most dynamic and challenging domains within artificial intelligence, primarily due to the inherent complexities of human language. Ambiguity, context sensitivity, and the vast diversity of languages pose significant hurdles for AI systems. Despite remarkable advancements, addressing these challenges remains a focal point for ongoing research and development in NLP. Let's delve into these challenges and explore how AI is being leveraged to overcome them.

AMBIGUITY IN LANGUAGE

Language ambiguity arises at multiple levels, including lexical (words with multiple meanings), syntactic (sentence structure that can be interpreted in different ways), and semantic (sentences with the same structure but different meanings).

Approaches to Tackling Ambiguity: AI systems use sophisticated models to understand context and disambiguate meanings. For instance, word sense disambiguation algorithms help determine the correct meaning of a word based on its usage in a sentence. Deep learning models, particularly those employing attention mechanisms, excel at capturing the nuances necessary to resolve ambiguities by considering the broader context in which a word or phrase is used.

CONTEXT SENSITIVITY

The meaning of words and sentences can significantly change depending on the context, including the preceding text, the speaker's intent, or even cultural factors. Capturing and interpreting this context is crucial for accurate language understanding.

Contextual Models: Transformer-based models like BERT and GPT have made significant strides in handling context sensitivity. By pre-training on vast corpora of text, these models learn rich contextual representations of language, enabling them to infer meaning based on the surrounding text and broader discourse.

DIVERSITY OF HUMAN LANGUAGE

The diversity of human language, with thousands of languages and dialects, each with its own grammar, syntax, and idioms, presents another layer of complexity. This diversity challenges NLP systems not only in understanding and generating language but also in scaling solutions across languages.

Cross-Linguistic Models and Transfer Learning: To address language diversity, researchers are developing multilingual models capable of understanding multiple languages. Transfer learning, where a model trained on one language is adapted to another, is also a promising approach. Models like mBERT (multilingual BERT) and XLM-R (Cross-lingual Language Model - RoBERTa) demonstrate the potential for cross-linguistic NLP applications.

OVERCOMING CHALLENGES WITH ADVANCED TECHNIQUES

Neural Machine Translation (NMT): NMT models have significantly improved the quality of machine translation by learning to translate text in a more nuanced and context-aware manner, addressing the challenge of linguistic diversity.

Sentiment Analysis and Emotion AI: By combining NLP with emotion AI, systems can better understand the emotional content of language, helping to resolve ambiguities related to emotional expressions and enhancing interactions with chatbots and virtual assistants.

Knowledge Graphs and Semantic Web: Integrating NLP with knowledge graphs and the semantic web helps machines understand the relationships between different concepts and entities in language, improving their ability to deal with ambiguity and context.

CONCLUSION

The challenges presented by ambiguity, context sensitivity, and the diversity of human language are significant but not insurmountable. Through the continuous advancement of AI and NLP technologies, including deep learning models and innovative approaches like transfer learning and knowledge integration, AI is becoming increasingly adept at navigating the complexities of human language. These advancements not only enhance the capabilities of NLP applications but also promise to bridge the gap between human and machine communication, making AI interactions more natural and intuitive.

MORE THAN JUST SMALL TALK

The journey of chatbots and virtual assistants from their inception as simple rule-based systems to today's advanced AI-driven entities illustrates the rapid evolution of artificial intelligence and natural language processing technologies. This progression has transformed chatbots and virtual assistants into versatile tools capable of engaging in meaningful conversations and performing a wide array of complex tasks, significantly enhancing user experience across various domains.

THE EARLY DAYS: RULE-BASED SYSTEMS

The earliest chatbots were rule-based systems that operated on a set of predefined rules or decision trees. These chatbots could only respond to specific inputs with pre-programmed responses. ELIZA, created in the mid-1960s, is one of the most famous early chatbots, simulating a psychotherapist by rephrasing many of the user's statements as questions. While these systems were ground-breaking at the time, their inability to understand context or handle unanticipated queries limited their usefulness and made conversations feel mechanical and repetitive.

THE INTRODUCTION OF MACHINE LEARNING

The introduction of machine learning into chatbot and virtual assistant development marked a significant advancement. Machine learning allowed these systems to learn from interactions, improving their ability to understand and respond to user queries over time. This shift from rule-based to learning-based systems enabled chatbots and virtual assistants to handle a broader range of questions and provide more relevant, personalized responses.

THE ERA OF NLP AND DEEP LEARNING

The integration of advanced natural language processing (NLP) and deep learning technologies further revolutionized chatbots and virtual assistants. NLP advancements, particularly in understanding context and user intent, coupled with deep learning's ability to process and learn from vast amounts of data, significantly enhanced the conversational abilities of these systems.

Contextual Understanding: Modern chatbots and virtual assistants can remember the context of a conversation and maintain the thread of discussion, making interactions more natural and fluid.

Personalization: AI-driven systems can now personalize interactions by learning from user preferences and behaviours, tailoring responses, and anticipating needs based on past interactions.

ADVANCED AI MODELS: TRANSFORMERS AND BEYOND

The advent of transformer models like BERT and GPT-3 has pushed the boundaries of what's possible with chatbots and virtual assistants. These models, which excel at generating human-like text and understanding nuanced language, have enabled the creation of chatbots and virtual assistants that can engage in complex conversations, understand abstract concepts, and even exhibit a form of creativity in their responses.

Enhanced Capabilities: Today's virtual assistants are not just confined to answering questions but can perform a wide range of tasks, from managing schedules and sending emails to controlling smart home devices and providing real-time translations.

Emotional Intelligence: Emerging models are beginning to incorporate emotional intelligence, allowing chatbots and virtual assistants to detect and respond to the emotional state of the user, further enhancing the conversational experience.

CONCLUSION

The evolution from simple rule-based chatbots to today's sophisticated AI-driven virtual assistants reflects the tremendous strides made in AI, machine learning, and NLP. As these technologies continue to advance, we can expect chatbots and virtual assistants to become even more integral to our daily lives, offering unprecedented levels of convenience, personalization, and interactive engagement. The future of these technologies promises not only to enhance how we interact with machines but also to redefine the possibilities of human-computer interaction.

EXAMPLES OF HOW CHATBOTS AND VIRTUAL ASSISTANTS ARE USED

Chatbots and virtual assistants, powered by advancements in artificial intelligence (AI) and natural language processing (NLP), have found widespread application across various sectors, notably transforming customer service, healthcare, and education. These AI-driven tools are not just enhancing efficiency and accessibility but are also providing highly personalized experiences. Let's explore some examples of their impact across these domains.

CUSTOMER SERVICE

In customer service, chatbots and virtual assistants are revolutionizing the way businesses interact with their customers, offering 24/7 support and significantly reducing wait times for queries.

Instant Support: Virtual assistants on websites and social media platforms can instantly respond to customer inquiries, from tracking orders to resolving common issues, without the need for human intervention. This immediacy improves customer satisfaction and loyalty.

Personalized Recommendations: AI-driven chatbots can analyze a customer's purchase history and preferences to offer personalized product recommendations, enhancing the shopping experience and boosting sales.

HEALTHCARE

The healthcare sector has seen remarkable benefits from the integration of chatbots and virtual assistants, particularly in improving patient engagement and streamlining care delivery.

Symptom Checkers: AI-powered chatbots can conduct preliminary symptom assessments, guiding patients to appropriate care based on their inputs. This not only helps in triaging but also ensures that patients receive timely medical advice.

Mental Health Support: Virtual assistants are being used to provide mental health support, offering coping mechanisms and mindfulness exercises to users. They can also remind patients to take their medication and follow their treatment plans, improving adherence and outcomes.

EDUCATION

In education, chatbots and virtual assistants are facilitating personalized learning experiences and providing administrative support, making education more accessible and engaging.

Personalized Tutoring: AI-driven educational chatbots can adapt to each student's learning pace and style, offering customized tutoring and feedback. This personalized approach helps in identifying knowledge gaps and enhancing the learning experience.

Administrative Assistance: Virtual assistants are used by educational institutions to handle administrative tasks, such as answering frequently asked questions about courses, admissions, and campus facilities. This frees up human resources to focus on more complex queries and improves the efficiency of administrative processes.

CONCLUSION

Chatbots and virtual assistants are making significant strides in customer service, healthcare, and education, among other fields. By providing round-the-clock support, personalized interactions, and accessibility, these AI-driven tools are not only enhancing efficiency but also transforming user experiences. As AI technology continues to evolve, the potential for chatbots and virtual assistants to further impact various sectors is immense, promising even more innovative applications and solutions tailored to meet the needs of users worldwide.

FUTURE OF CONVERSATIONAL AI

The future of conversational AI holds immense promise, with advancements poised to redefine the depth and quality of interactions between humans and machines. As technology evolves, we're looking at a horizon where chatbots and virtual assistants will not only understand and generate human language more effectively but also engage in empathetic, context-aware conversations that closely mimic human interaction. However, this future also brings forth ethical considerations that must be addressed to ensure the responsible development and deployment of conversational AI.

EMPATHETIC AND CONTEXT-AWARE INTERACTIONS

EMOTIONAL INTELLIGENCE

The next frontier for conversational AI involves integrating emotional intelligence, enabling systems to recognize, interpret, and respond to human emotions. By analysing vocal cues, language patterns, and even facial expressions (in video interactions), AI could offer responses that are not just contextually appropriate but also emotionally resonant, providing comfort, encouragement, or empathy as needed.

ADVANCED CONTEXT UNDERSTANDING

Future advancements will likely see conversational AI becoming more adept at understanding the context of interactions, including the user's background, the conversation's history, and external factors influencing the dialogue. This level of context awareness will allow for more nuanced and relevant conversations, enhancing user satisfaction and engagement.

ETHICAL CONSIDERATIONS

As conversational AI becomes more integrated into daily life, several ethical considerations emerge, necessitating careful attention and proactive measures.

PRIVACY AND DATA SECURITY

The ability of conversational AI to understand and empathize with users will largely depend on access to personal data. Ensuring the privacy and security of this data is paramount. Users must have control over what data is collected and how it's used, with transparent policies and robust data protection measures in place.

BIAS AND FAIRNESS

AI systems learn from data, which means they can inherit biases present in that data. As conversational AI becomes more sophisticated, ensuring that these systems do not perpetuate or amplify biases is crucial. This requires diverse training data, ongoing monitoring for biased outcomes, and mechanisms to correct biases when identified.

DEPENDENCE AND DEHUMANIZATION

There's a potential risk that increased reliance on conversational AI for social interaction could lead to dehumanization or reduced human contact, particularly affecting vulnerable populations like the elderly. Balancing the benefits of AI companionship with the need for human connection will be essential.

TRANSPARENCY AND ACCOUNTABILITY

As conversational AI systems make more decisions and take actions on behalf of users, establishing clear lines of transparency and accountability becomes critical. Users should understand how decisions are made and have recourse if outcomes are incorrect or harmful.

THE PATH FORWARD

The future of conversational AI is not just about technological advancements but also about navigating the ethical landscape that accompanies these innovations. Developing empathetic, context-aware conversational agents offers the potential to greatly enhance human-computer interaction, making technology more accessible and supportive. However, realizing this potential requires a commitment to ethical principles, ensuring that conversational AI serves to augment human experience positively, without compromising individual rights or societal values.

As we move forward, the collaboration between technologists, ethicists, policymakers, and users will be key in shaping a future where conversational AI enhances lives while adhering to the highest ethical standards.

BREAKING DOWN OF LANGUAGE BARRIERS

Machine translation (MT) has been a pivotal area in computational linguistics, aiming to break down language barriers and facilitate seamless communication across different languages. The evolution of MT from statistical methods to neural machine translation (NMT) has brought about significant improvements in translation accuracy, fluency, and the overall quality of translated text. Let's explore this progression and its impact on global communication.

STATISTICAL MACHINE TRANSLATION (SMT)

Statistical Machine Translation, which dominated the field until the mid-2010s, relies on statistical models to translate text from one language to another. These models are built upon analyses of bilingual text corpora, where the system learns translations based on the probability of certain words and phrases being equivalent in the source and target languages.

How It Works: SMT uses algorithms to align segments of the source and target texts in a parallel corpus, learning translations at the word, phrase, and sometimes sentence level. The translation process involves decoding, where the system generates multiple possible translations and selects the most probable one based on learned statistical models.

Limitations: While SMT marked a significant advancement in MT, it struggled with maintaining context over longer texts and managing the syntactic and grammatical differences between languages. This often resulted in translations that were technically correct but lacked natural fluency and coherence.

NEURAL MACHINE TRANSLATION (NMT)

The advent of Neural Machine Translation represented a paradigm shift, leveraging deep learning and neural network architectures to model the entire translation process. NMT systems learn to translate by directly mapping sequences of text from the source language to the target language, improving both accuracy and fluency.

How It Works: NMT uses a sequence-to-sequence (seq2seq) model, typically consisting of an encoder that processes the source text and a decoder that generates the translation. This approach allows the model to consider the entire input sentence, capturing long-range dependencies and contextual nuances more effectively than SMT.

Advancements: The introduction of attention mechanisms and later, transformer models, further enhanced NMT's capabilities. These innovations allow the system to focus on relevant parts of the input sentence as needed throughout the translation process, significantly improving the quality of translations, especially for languages with substantial syntactic differences.

IMPACT ON ACCURACY AND FLUENCY

The shift to NMT has led to remarkable improvements in the quality of machine translations:

Increased Accuracy: NMT provides more accurate translations by better understanding the context and nuances of the source text, leading to fewer errors and more precise translations.

Enhanced Fluency: Translations produced by NMT systems are more fluent and natural-sounding, closely resembling human-generated text. This is particularly evident in languages with flexible word order, where NMT excels in producing coherent and grammatically correct sentences.

Handling of Idiomatic Expressions: NMT has shown a better grasp of idiomatic expressions and colloquial language, translating such phrases in a way that captures their intended meaning more effectively than SMT.

CONCLUSION

The evolution from statistical machine translation to neural machine translation has significantly advanced the field, making machine translation more accessible, accurate, and user-friendly. These advancements have not only improved cross-cultural communication but have also opened up vast amounts of information across languages, contributing to a more connected and informed world. As NMT continues to evolve, we can expect further breakthroughs that will continue to diminish language barriers.

IMPACT OF MACHINE TRANSLATION

Machine translation (MT) has profoundly impacted global communication, business, and education, serving as a pivotal tool in bridging language divides and fostering cross-cultural exchanges. By enabling the instantaneous translation of text and speech across numerous languages, MT has democratized access to information, opened new markets, and enhanced educational opportunities worldwide. Let's delve into the specifics of these impacts.

GLOBAL COMMUNICATION

MT has significantly facilitated cross-cultural communication, allowing individuals from different linguistic backgrounds to interact seamlessly. Social media platforms, forums, and messaging apps increasingly integrate MT, enabling users to understand and engage with content in languages other than their own. This has not only promoted cultural exchange but also fostered international collaboration and understanding.

Emergency Response and Aid: In disaster or crisis situations, MT plays a crucial role in breaking down language barriers, ensuring that vital information reaches everyone affected, regardless of language.

BUSINESS AND COMMERCE

In the realm of global business, MT has been a game-changer, enabling companies to easily cross linguistic boundaries that once posed significant challenges.

Market Expansion: Businesses can now reach a global audience with minimal effort, translating websites, product listings, and marketing materials into multiple languages. This accessibility has opened up new markets and customer bases for companies of all sizes.

Customer Support: MT allows for real-time customer support across different languages, improving service and customer satisfaction. Companies can provide FAQs, support documents, and live chat services in multiple languages, enhancing the customer experience and building loyalty.

EDUCATION

MT has had a transformative impact on education by making learning materials and scholarly work accessible across languages, thus democratizing education and knowledge.

Access to Diverse Resources: Students and educators can access a vast array of educational materials, research papers, and courses in languages other than their own, broadening their learning opportunities and perspectives.

Language Learning: While not a substitute for language learning, MT serves as a valuable tool for learners to understand content in target languages and practice translation skills, thereby supporting language acquisition.

DEMOCRATIZATION OF INFORMATION

Perhaps one of the most significant impacts of MT is the democratization of access to information. By breaking down language barriers, MT has made information, once siloed by language, universally accessible.

Knowledge Sharing: People worldwide can access news, scientific research, legal documents, and more in their native languages, promoting global knowledge sharing and collaboration.

Empowerment through Information: Access to information is a key driver of empowerment and development. MT enables individuals to access health information, legal rights, educational resources, and more, regardless of the language in which such information is originally published.

CONCLUSION

Machine translation has emerged as a cornerstone technology in our increasingly interconnected world, facilitating cross-cultural exchange, expanding business opportunities, and enhancing educational outcomes. By democratizing access to information, MT empowers individuals and communities, fostering a more inclusive global dialogue. As MT technology continues to advance, its role in promoting global understanding and cooperation is expected to grow, further embedding it as an essential tool in overcoming linguistic and cultural barriers.

CHALLENGES REMAINING IN MACHINE TRANSLATION

Machine translation (MT) has made significant strides in breaking down language barriers and facilitating global communication. However, several challenges remain, particularly in translating low-resource languages and preserving cultural nuances. These challenges highlight the complexity of language and the intricacies involved in capturing its full essence through automated systems. Let's explore these challenges and the ongoing efforts to address them.

TRANSLATING LOW-RESOURCE LANGUAGES

Low-resource languages, those with limited available data, especially digital text and translations, pose a significant challenge for MT systems. The performance of modern MT, particularly neural machine translation (NMT), relies heavily on large datasets for training. The scarcity of such data for many languages limits the effectiveness of MT in providing accurate and reliable translations.

EFFORTS TO ADDRESS THE CHALLENGE:

Data Collection and Sharing: Initiatives aimed at collecting and sharing linguistic data for low-resource languages are underway, involving collaboration between governments, academic institutions, and communities.

Transfer Learning: This approach leverages models trained on high-resource languages to improve translation quality for low-resource languages, adapting the knowledge gained from one language to another.

Unsupervised and Semi-supervised Learning: These methods can learn from unaligned text, reducing the reliance on large parallel corpora. By leveraging monolingual data, which is more abundant, these approaches can enhance translations for low-resource languages.

PRESERVING CULTURAL NUANCES

Language is deeply intertwined with culture, carrying nuances, idioms, and references that are often challenging to translate accurately. Preserving these cultural nuances is crucial for translations that are not only linguistically accurate but also culturally resonant.

CHALLENGES IN CULTURAL NUANCE PRESERVATION:

Idioms and Expressions: Many languages contain idioms and expressions with no direct equivalents in other languages, making literal translations misleading or nonsensical.

Cultural References: References to historical events, literary works, or cultural practices can be obscure to outsiders, requiring additional context for accurate translation.

Contextual and Cultural Awareness: Advanced NMT systems are being developed to incorporate broader contextual and cultural awareness, allowing for translations that consider not just the text but also the cultural and situational context.

Human-in-the-loop: Combining AI with human expertise, where translators review and refine machine-generated translations, ensures that cultural nuances are preserved. This approach leverages the efficiency of MT while benefiting from the cultural sensitivity of human translators.

Cross-lingual Embeddings: These represent words or phrases from different languages in a shared semantic space, helping to capture deeper meanings and cultural nuances by understanding the relationships between concepts across languages.

CONCLUSION

While machine translation has dramatically improved access to information and communication across languages, translating low-resource languages and preserving cultural nuances remain significant challenges. Addressing these issues requires not only technological innovation but also collaborative efforts that leverage both human expertise and advanced AI. By focusing on these challenges, the field of MT can continue to advance, offering more inclusive and culturally sensitive translations that bridge languages and cultures more effectively.

CHAPTER 6: AI IN THE WORLD OF ART AND CREATIVITY

COLLABORATION BETWEEN MAN AND MACHINE

The integration of Artificial Intelligence (AI) in creative fields has led to fascinating collaborations between humans and machines, challenging our traditional notions of creativity and artistic authorship. Here, we examine case studies across music, art, and literature that highlight the dynamic interplay between human ingenuity and AI's computational power.

AI IN MUSIC: AIVA AND TARYN SOUTHERN

Case Study: AIVA (Artificial Intelligence Virtual Artist) is an AI composer that has been trained on thousands of pieces of classical music to create original compositions. AIVA's music has been performed by orchestras and used in soundtracks for films and games.

Collaboration Example: Taryn Southern, a YouTube artist, collaborated with AIVA to produce an entire album titled "I AM AI," where the music was composed by AI, and Southern provided the vocals. This collaboration showcased how AI can be used as a tool to extend the creative capabilities of human artists, allowing them to explore new musical landscapes.

AI IN ART: REFIK ANADOL AND "MACHINE HALLUCINATION"

Case Study: Refik Anadol is a media artist known for using AI in his installations. One of his notable works, "Machine Hallucination," is a large-scale AI-driven public art installation that uses GANs (Generative Adversarial Networks) to create stunning visual experiences. The artwork is based on a vast dataset of images of New York City, which the AI uses to generate abstract visual narratives.

Collaboration Example: Anadol's work exemplifies the collaboration between human artistic vision and AI's generative capabilities. By feeding the AI system specific datasets and guiding the algorithm's output, Anadol creates art that is both a reflection of the machine's "hallucinations" and his creative direction, blurring the lines between the artist and the tool.

AI IN LITERATURE: "SUNSPRING" AND AI-WRITTEN NOVELS

Case Study: "Sunspring" is a short science fiction film with a script entirely generated by an AI named Benjamin. The AI was fed hundreds of sci-fi TV and movie scripts to learn the genre's conventions, after which it produced an original script. The film's human creators then interpreted and filmed it, bringing the AI's narrative to life.

Collaboration Example: The creation of "Sunspring" demonstrates a unique form of collaboration where the AI generates the foundational text, and human artists interpret and realize the vision through their creative lens. This process highlights the potential of AI to contribute original ideas and narratives, which human creativity can then shape and contextualize.

CONCLUSION

These case studies illustrate the vast potential of AI as a collaborator in the creative process, offering new tools and methodologies for music, art, and literature. The interaction between human artists and AI systems is not a one-way process but a dialogue—a continuous exchange of inputs and refinements that enriches the creative outcome. As AI technologies evolve, so too will the nature of this collaboration, promising even more innovative and boundary-pushing works of art that challenge our understanding of creativity.

IMPACT OF AI ON CREATIVITY AND ARTISTIC EXPRESSION

The impact of Artificial Intelligence (AI) on creativity and artistic expression is a topic of both fascination and debate within the artistic community and beyond. As AI systems become increasingly capable of generating music, art, literature, and other forms of creative work, questions arise about the nature of creativity itself and whether AI can possess it or merely mimics human creative processes. This discussion touches on philosophical, psychological, and technological perspectives.

AI AND THE NATURE OF CREATIVITY

Creativity, traditionally seen as a uniquely human trait, involves the ability to generate ideas, solutions, or works that are both novel and appropriate. AI's role in creativity challenges this notion, presenting a paradigm where machines can produce work that, to some extent, meets these criteria.

Generative Capabilities: AI, particularly through generative models like GANs (Generative Adversarial Networks) and transformer-based models, can produce new content that often surprises and inspires human audiences. These models can identify patterns and relationships in vast datasets that humans cannot easily discern, leading to the creation of unique and innovative outputs.

Mimicking Human Creativity: Critics argue that AI's creative process is fundamentally different from human creativity. AI systems generate outputs based on the data they are trained on, using algorithms to optimize for certain criteria. This process, some say, is more akin to mimicry than genuine creativity, as it lacks intentionality, consciousness, and emotional engagement—elements often associated with human creative acts.

THE IMPACT ON ARTISTIC EXPRESSION

The integration of AI into the creative process has undeniably expanded the tools available to artists, offering new ways to explore and express artistic visions.

Collaboration Between Man and Machine: Many artists view AI as a collaborative partner that can enhance their creative expression. AI can process and analyze data in ways that humans cannot, providing artists with new insights and inspirations. This collaboration can lead to hybrid works that combine the best of human intuition and emotional depth with AI's computational power and novelty.

Accessibility and Democratization: AI tools can lower barriers to creative expression, allowing individuals without traditional artistic training to explore their creativity. This democratization of creativity has the potential to enrich the cultural landscape with diverse voices and perspectives.

ETHICAL AND PHILOSOPHICAL CONSIDERATIONS

The rise of AI in creative domains also raises ethical and philosophical questions about authorship, authenticity, and the value of art.

Authorship and Ownership: When AI generates art, questions arise about who the author is—the creator of the AI, the operator of the system, or the AI itself? This has implications for copyright and the recognition of creative contributions.

Authenticity and Emotional Connection: Some argue that art created by AI lacks the authenticity of human-made art, as it does not originate from personal experience or emotion. This perspective suggests that while AI can produce aesthetically pleasing works, it cannot replicate the emotional depth and connection that often give art its value.

CONCLUSION

The impact of AI on creativity and artistic expression is profound and multifaceted, challenging our traditional understandings of creativity and prompting us to reconsider the boundaries between human and machine capabilities. While AI can generate novel and innovative works, the debate over whether it can be truly creative or merely mimics human creativity reflects broader questions about the nature of consciousness, intentionality, and what it means to be creative. As AI technology continues to evolve, so too will its role in the arts, potentially leading to new forms of creative expression that transcend current limitations and definitions.

ETHICAL CONSIDERATIONS AND COPYRIGHT IMPLICATIONS OF AI-GENERATED ART AND LITERATURE.

The rise of AI-generated art and literature has sparked a complex debate surrounding ethical considerations and copyright implications. As AI systems become increasingly capable of producing creative works, questions about ownership, authorship, and the moral rights of AI versus human creators have come to the forefront. These issues challenge existing legal frameworks and ethical norms, necessitating a re-evaluation of how we understand and protect creative works.

ETHICAL CONSIDERATIONS

Authenticity and Originality: There's an ongoing debate about the authenticity and originality of AI-generated works. Can a piece of art created by an algorithm be considered original, or is it merely a derivative work based on the data it was trained on? This raises ethical questions about the value we assign to AI-generated art compared to human-created art.

Transparency: There's a need for transparency regarding the use of AI in creating art. Artists and creators who use AI as a tool in their creative process should disclose its involvement, allowing audiences to make informed judgments about the work's context and origins.

COPYRIGHT IMPLICATIONS

Copyright law traditionally protects the original works of authorship by human creators, leaving a grey area when it comes to AI-generated content. The main question revolves around who, if anyone, holds the copyright to works created by AI:

AI as a Tool: If AI is considered a tool used by a human artist, then the human creator could be recognized as the author, holding the copyright to the work. This is akin to using a sophisticated camera for photography; the photographer owns the copyright to the images produced.

AI as the Creator: If an AI system autonomously generates a piece of art or music without direct human input, determining copyright ownership becomes more challenging. Current copyright laws in many jurisdictions do not recognize AI as an author, leaving such works potentially in the public domain or under the ownership of the AI's developer or operator.

ONGOING EFFORTS AND PROPOSALS

Legislative Reforms: Some jurisdictions are considering reforms to copyright laws to address the challenges posed by AI-generated works. These reforms could involve creating new categories of copyright that recognize the role of AI while ensuring that human creators who contribute to or guide the AI process are protected.

Creative Commons for AI: Another proposal is the development of a Creative Commons-like framework specifically for AI-generated content, which would allow creators to specify the terms under which their AI-generated works can be used, shared, or modified.

CONCLUSION

The ethical considerations and copyright implications of AI-generated art and literature present a complex challenge that intersects with questions of creativity, authorship, and the role of AI in society. As AI continues to evolve and become more integrated into the creative process, it will be crucial for legal systems, creators, and society at large to develop frameworks that recognize the contributions of both humans and AI. These frameworks must balance the protection of creative works with the encouragement of innovation and the sharing of culture in the digital age.

CREATING NEW CONTENT

Generative AI technologies have revolutionized the creation of new content across various domains, including art, music, literature, and more. At the heart of this revolution are Generative Adversarial Networks (GANs) and transformer models, which have distinct mechanisms for generating novel content. Understanding these technologies provides insight into how AI can be both a creator and an innovator.

GENERATIVE ADVERSARIAL NETWORKS (GANS)

GANs are a class of machine learning frameworks introduced by Ian Goodfellow and his colleagues in 2014. They consist of two neural networks, the generator and the discriminator, which are trained simultaneously through adversarial processes.

How GANs Work: The generator creates new data instances (such as images), while the discriminator evaluates them against a set of real data, trying to distinguish genuine instances from the fakes. The generator aims to produce data so convincing that the discriminator cannot tell them apart from real instances. This process continues until the generator produces high-quality outputs.

Application in Artistic Content Creation: In the realm of art, GANs have been used to generate realistic images, artworks that mimic the styles of famous painters, and even entirely new visual forms that no human has ever created. Projects like DeepArt and This Person Does Not Exist showcase the power of GANs in creating visually compelling content that blurs the line between human-made and machine-generated art.

TRANSFORMERS

Transformers, introduced in the paper "Attention is All You Need" by Vaswani et al., represent a breakthrough in handling sequential data, surpassing the capabilities of previous models like RNNs and LSTMs, particularly in natural language processing (NLP).

How Transformers Work: Unlike models that process data sequentially, transformers use self-attention mechanisms to weigh the importance of different parts of the input data. This allows them to consider the entire context of the input at once, making them exceptionally good at understanding the nuances of language.

Application in Creative Writing and Beyond: Transformer models like GPT (Generative Pre-trained Transformer) have been used to write coherent and contextually relevant text, including stories, poems, and even news articles. GPT-3, with its vast training dataset and sophisticated understanding of language, can generate text that is often indistinguishable from that written by humans. Beyond text, transformers are also being explored for generating music and code, showcasing their versatility in creative content generation.

THE CREATIVE PROCESS WITH GENERATIVE AI

The use of GANs and transformers in creating new content involves both the autonomous generation of novel outputs and the curation by human artists or creators. This collaborative process between AI and humans allows for the exploration of new creative territories, where AI's capacity to generate unprecedented forms and ideas meets human creativity and emotional depth.

Human-AI Collaboration: Artists and creators often use generative AI as a tool in their creative process, leveraging AI-generated content as inspiration or as elements within their works. This collaboration can result in artworks, music, and literature that are truly novel, pushing the boundaries of traditional creative practices.

CONCLUSION

Generative AI technologies like GANs and transformers are at the forefront of creating new artistic content, offering tools that can generate novel and complex outputs across various mediums. As these technologies continue to evolve, they promise to further expand the possibilities of creative expression, enabling artists and creators to explore new horizons in art, literature, and beyond. The future of generative AI in creativity is not just about the technology itself but also about how it integrates with human imagination and artistic practices, creating a new paradigm for artistic creation.

GENERATIVE AI IN ACTION

Generative AI has made remarkable strides in various creative fields, producing work that spans from visual arts to literature, often blurring the lines between human and machine creativity. Here are some notable examples of generative

AI in action, showcasing the technology's ability to mimic historical art styles, compose literature, and more.

AI-GENERATED PAINTINGS

DeepArt: Utilizing deep neural networks, DeepArt transforms photographs into artworks mimicking the styles of famous painters like Van Gogh, Picasso, and Turner. Users can upload a photo, choose an art style, and the AI generates a unique piece of art by applying the stylistic features of the chosen genre to the photo.

The Next Rembrandt: A project that combined data from Rembrandt's paintings with deep learning algorithms to create a new artwork that closely resembles the style of the Dutch master. The AI analysed Rembrandt's use of geometry, composition, and painting materials to produce a piece that could easily pass as one of his undiscovered works.

AI-WRITTEN NOVELS AND POETRY

"1 the Road" by Ross Goodwin: In this experimental project, AI equipped with cameras, GPS, and a microphone was placed in a car traveling across the country. The AI, using these inputs, wrote a novel in real-time. The text reflects the landscapes, conversations, and experiences encountered along the journey, showcasing a unique blend of travelogue and AI-generated literature.

GPT-3 Poetry: OpenAI's GPT-3 has been used to write poems that range from sonnets to free verse. By feeding the model prompts or styles, users have coaxed out verses that are surprisingly profound, nuanced, and stylistically diverse, demonstrating the AI's ability to mimic a wide range of poetic voices and themes.

AI IN MUSIC COMPOSITION

AIVA (Artificial Intelligence Virtual Artist): AIVA is an AI composer that has created original compositions in the style of classical music, which have been performed by human orchestras. AIVA analyses the works of classical composers to understand patterns and structures in music, then generates new compositions that reflect these learned styles.

Daddy's Car: Developed by Sony's CSL Research Laboratory, this song was composed by AI in the style of The Beatles. The AI analysed a large dataset of songs from the iconic band to understand their specific sound and produced a new track that captures the essence of their music.

"Sunspring": A short science fiction film written entirely by an AI named Benjamin. The script was generated by feeding the AI hundreds of sci-fi TV and movie scripts, from which it learned to craft its own screenplay. The result is a surreal and intriguing narrative that offers a glimpse into the potential of AI in screenwriting.

CONCLUSION

These examples illustrate the breadth and depth of generative AI's capabilities in the realm of art and creativity. From creating paintings in the styles of historical masters to composing music and writing novels and poetry, AI is opening new avenues for creative expression. While the debate continues about whether AI can truly be creative or is simply mimicking human creativity, these instances highlight the potential for AI to serve as a powerful tool and collaborator in the creative process. As generative AI technologies evolve, we can expect to see even more innovative and boundary-pushing works that challenge our perceptions of art and authorship.

ROLE OF HUMAN INPUT AND OVERSIGHT IN THE GENERATIVE PROCESS

The integration of Artificial Intelligence (AI) in creative processes has opened new horizons in art, literature, and music, among other fields. However, the role of human input and oversight remains crucial in guiding the generative process of AI to ensure meaningful, ethical, and innovative outcomes. This human involvement is pivotal at various stages, from the selection of training data to the fine-tuning of AI models and the interpretation of their outputs.

SELECTION OF TRAINING DATA

The selection of training data is a foundational step that significantly influences the behaviour and output of generative AI models. This phase requires careful consideration and human judgment to ensure the data is representative, diverse, and free from biases that could skew the AI's creations.

Curating Diverse and Inclusive Data Sets: Human curators play a vital role in assembling datasets that reflect a wide range of styles, cultures, and perspectives. This diversity in training data helps prevent the perpetuation of stereotypes and biases in AI-generated content.

Ethical Considerations: Humans must also consider the ethical implications of the data used to train AI models. This includes respecting copyright laws and ensuring that the data does not contain harmful or offensive material.

FINE-TUNING AI MODELS

Once an AI model has been trained, fine-tuning it for specific creative tasks often requires human expertise and intuition. This process adjusts the model's parameters to better align with the desired artistic or creative goals.

Guiding Creative Direction: Artists and creators work with AI models, adjusting settings and providing feedback to steer the AI towards producing outputs that align with their creative vision. This collaboration ensures that the AI's generative capabilities are harnessed in a way that complements human creativity.

Iterative Refinement: The fine-tuning process is typically iterative, with humans evaluating the AI's outputs and making adjustments to the model as needed. This hands-on involvement is crucial for achieving high-quality, nuanced, and contextually appropriate results.

INTERPRETATION AND CURATION OF OUTPUTS

The interpretation of AI-generated content often requires human insight to assess its relevance, quality, and artistic merit. This stage is where the collaborative nature of human-AI creativity is most evident.

Curation and Selection: Not all AI-generated content meets the intended creative standards or objectives. Humans play a key role in curating and selecting the outputs that best represent their artistic goals, sometimes combining or modifying them to create the final piece.

Adding Context and Meaning: Human creators provide context and meaning to AI-generated works, interpreting them in ways that resonate with audiences. This may involve integrating AI-generated elements into larger works, providing narratives that frame or explain the AI's creations, or using the AI's output as a starting point for further artistic exploration.

CONCLUSION

The role of human input and oversight in the generative process of AI is indispensable for ensuring that the technology serves as an effective and ethical tool for creative expression. By carefully selecting training data, fine-tuning models, and curating outputs, humans guide AI to produce works that are not only innovative and surprising but also meaningful and aligned with broader artistic and cultural values. As AI continues to evolve, the collaborative synergy between human creativity and machine intelligence will undoubtedly lead to even more profound and impactful forms of art and expression.

POTENTIAL AND PITFALLS

The future of creative AI holds immense promise, with the potential to further revolutionize the arts and expand the boundaries of human creativity. As technology advances, we stand on the brink of a new era where AI not only assists in the creative process but also challenges our understanding of creativity itself. However, this future also presents significant pitfalls that need careful consideration. Let's explore the potential advancements and the dual-edged nature of creative AI's impact on the arts.

TECHNOLOGICAL POTENTIAL AND CREATIVE POSSIBILITIES

Enhanced Collaborative Creativity: Future advancements in AI could lead to more sophisticated collaborative tools that augment human creativity, allowing artists to explore new realms of expression. Imagine AI partners that can anticipate an artist's needs, suggest alternative creative paths, or even inspire new ideas based on emerging trends or historical data.

Expanding the Scope of Creativity: As AI becomes capable of understanding and replicating more complex artistic styles and techniques, it could unlock new forms of art that are currently unimaginable. This includes blending different mediums, styles, and cultural elements to create hybrid works that transcend traditional categories.

Democratization of Artistic Expression: Creative AI has the potential to lower barriers to artistic expression, making tools and techniques accessible to a broader audience. This democratization could lead to a surge in creativity and innovation, as people from diverse backgrounds bring their unique perspectives to the arts.

PITFALLS AND CHALLENGES

Authenticity and Originality Concerns: As AI-generated art becomes more prevalent, questions about the authenticity and originality of creative works may arise. Distinguishing between human-created art and AI-generated art could become challenging, potentially impacting the value and perception of artistic works.

Ethical and Copyright Issues: The use of AI in creating art raises complex ethical and copyright issues, particularly regarding the ownership of AI-generated works and the use of copyrighted material as training data. Navigating these legal landscapes will be crucial as creative AI evolves.

Overreliance on Technology: There's a risk that reliance on AI for creative processes could lead to a homogenization of art or a devaluation of human creativity. Ensuring that AI serves as a tool for enhancing human creativity, rather than replacing it, will be essential.

NAVIGATING THE FUTURE

Balancing Human and Machine Creativity: The future of creative AI should strive for a balance where AI enhances human creativity without overshadowing it. Cultivating an environment where humans and AI collaborate, each contributing their unique strengths, could lead to a richer, more diverse artistic landscape.

Ethical Development and Use: Developing creative AI ethically, with consideration for copyright, data privacy, and the impact on human artists, will be paramount. This includes transparent use of data, respecting intellectual property rights, and ensuring equitable access to AI tools.

Embracing New Artistic Identities: The arts community and society at large may need to embrace new definitions of artistic identity and creativity that include AI as a collaborator. This could involve rethinking how we value and define art, moving towards a model that recognizes the contribution of both human and machine.

CONCLUSION

The future of creative AI is fraught with both potential and pitfalls. Technological advancements promise to unlock new creative possibilities, transforming the arts in ways we have yet to fully comprehend. However, navigating this future will require careful consideration of ethical, legal, and societal implications. By addressing these challenges head-on, we can ensure that creative AI serves to enrich human creativity, fostering an artistic renaissance that celebrates the synergy between human and machine intelligence.

POTENTIAL PITFALLS AND CHALLENGES OF CREATIVE AI

The integration of Artificial Intelligence (AI) into creative fields has sparked both excitement and apprehension. While the potential for AI to enhance and expand the boundaries of human creativity is immense, there are significant pitfalls and challenges that accompany its adoption. These concerns range from the devaluation of human artistry and potential job losses to ethical considerations surrounding the use of AI in creating art. Addressing these challenges is crucial for ensuring that the evolution of creative AI benefits society as a whole.

DEVALUATION OF HUMAN ARTISTRY

One of the primary concerns is that AI-generated art might lead to the devaluation of human artistry. As AI becomes capable of producing works that rival or even surpass human-created art in complexity and appeal, there's a risk that the unique value and emotional depth of human-made art could be undermined.

Preserving Human Touch: It's essential to recognize and preserve the irreplaceable value of the human touch in art. The experiences, emotions, and personal stories that human artists bring to their work contribute to the art's depth and resonance, aspects that AI has yet to replicate fully.

LOSS OF JOBS IN CREATIVE INDUSTRIES

The automation of creative processes through AI raises concerns about job displacement within creative industries. As AI tools become more sophisticated, there's a potential for roles traditionally filled by humans, such as graphic design, music composition, and even writing, to be automated to some extent.

Augmentation, Not Replacement: Focusing on AI as a tool for augmentation rather than replacement can help mitigate job loss concerns. By leveraging AI to enhance their capabilities, creative professionals can explore new opportunities and roles that AI alone cannot fulfil.

ETHICAL USE OF AI IN CREATING ART

The ethical use of AI in art creation encompasses several issues, including copyright infringement, consent, and the transparency of AI's role in the creative process.

Copyright and Consent: AI systems often require large datasets for training, which may include copyrighted works. Ensuring that these systems are trained on ethically sourced, copyright-cleared materials is vital. Additionally, the consent of artists whose works are used to train AI models should be considered.

Transparency: Being transparent about the use of AI in the creation of art is crucial for maintaining trust and integrity in the arts. Audiences should be informed when AI has been used in the creative process, allowing them to appreciate the art within its proper context.

NAVIGATING THE CHALLENGES

To navigate these challenges, a multi-faceted approach is necessary:

Ethical Guidelines and Standards: Developing ethical guidelines and standards for the use of AI in creative processes can help address concerns about copyright, consent, and transparency.

Education and Reskilling: Providing education and reskilling opportunities for artists and creative professionals can help them adapt to the changing landscape, leveraging AI to enhance their work and discover new creative avenues.

Collaborative Creativity: Encouraging a collaborative view of AI in creativity, where AI is seen as a partner or tool rather than a competitor, can help preserve the value of human artistry and creativity.

CONCLUSION

The potential pitfalls and challenges of creative AI highlight the need for careful consideration and proactive measures to ensure that its development and use benefit society. By addressing concerns about the devaluation of human artistry, job displacement, and ethical issues, we can foster an environment where AI enhances human creativity, leading to a richer and more diverse artistic landscape.

POTENTIAL FOR AI TO DEMOCRATIZE ART AND CREATIVITY

The advent of Artificial Intelligence (AI) in the realm of art and creativity heralds a transformative shift, not just in how art is created, but also in who can create art. One of the most profound impacts of creative AI is its potential to democratize artistic expression, making it more accessible to a broader audience, including those without traditional artistic training or skills. This democratization could significantly alter the cultural and creative landscape, fostering a more inclusive environment for artistic expression.

LOWERING BARRIERS TO ENTRY

AI tools and platforms can lower the barriers to entry for artistic creation by providing intuitive interfaces and automating complex aspects of the creative process. For instance, AI-powered drawing and painting programs can assist users in refining sketches, suggesting colour palettes, or even completing parts of a composition, enabling individuals with limited drawing skills to bring their visions to life.

Generative Art Platforms: Platforms that use generative AI algorithms allow users to create complex and aesthetically pleasing artworks by inputting simple parameters or prompts. These platforms can generate music, visual art, poetry, and more, making the act of creation more about conceptualization and less about technical execution.

ENHANCING CREATIVITY THROUGH COLLABORATION

AI can act as a collaborative partner in the creative process, offering suggestions, generating ideas, and providing feedback. This collaboration can enhance human creativity, allowing creators to explore new directions and possibilities that they might not have considered on their own.

Creative Expansion: AI can analyze vast amounts of data to suggest novel combinations of styles, techniques, or themes, expanding the creative horizons of artists and enabling them to experiment with new ideas that push the boundaries of traditional art forms.

MAKING EDUCATION AND LEARNING MORE ACCESSIBLE

AI-driven platforms and tools can also make education in the arts more accessible, offering personalized learning experiences that adapt to the user's pace and style of learning. From virtual tutors in music and painting to AI systems that provide feedback on creative writing, AI can offer guidance and instruction to aspiring artists anywhere in the world.

Personalized Learning: AI systems can tailor educational content to the learner's interests and skill level, providing challenges that are neither too easy nor too difficult. This personalized approach can help maintain engagement and foster a deeper understanding of artistic techniques and concepts.

ETHICAL CONSIDERATIONS AND CHALLENGES

While the potential for AI to democratize art and creativity is significant, it also raises ethical considerations and challenges. Ensuring equitable access to AI tools and addressing issues related to copyright and the originality of AI-generated works are critical concerns that need to be addressed.

Equitable Access: As AI tools become more sophisticated, ensuring that they are accessible to everyone, regardless of socioeconomic status, is crucial for true democratization. This includes developing open-source platforms and affordable software that can be used by a wide audience.

Navigating Copyright and Originality: Clear guidelines and ethical standards are needed to navigate the complexities of copyright in AI-generated art, ensuring that creators are fairly credited and compensated for their work.

CONCLUSION

The potential for AI to democratize art and creativity is vast, offering exciting possibilities for expanding who can create art and how it is created. By making artistic expression more accessible and fostering a collaborative relationship between humans and machines, AI has the potential to enrich the cultural landscape with a diversity of voices and perspectives. However, realizing this potential will require careful consideration of the ethical and practical challenges that accompany the use of AI in creative endeavours.

CHAPTER 7: THE ROLE OF AI IN BUSINESS AND INDUSTRY

DIAGNOSIS, TREATMENT, AND RESEARCH

The integration of Artificial Intelligence (AI) into healthcare has marked a significant leap forward in diagnostic accuracy, treatment personalization, and medical research. Among its many applications, the use of machine learning algorithms in interpreting medical images such as X-rays, MRIs, and CT scans stands out for its potential to revolutionize patient diagnosis and outcomes. Let's delve into how AI is enhancing diagnostic accuracy and its implications for healthcare.

IMPROVING DIAGNOSTIC ACCURACY WITH AI

Machine Learning in Medical Imaging: Machine learning algorithms, particularly deep learning models like Convolutional Neural Networks (CNNs), have shown remarkable success in analysing medical images. These AI models are trained on vast datasets of annotated images to learn patterns and features associated with specific diseases or conditions. Once trained, they can identify these features in new images, often with equal or greater accuracy than human radiologists.

Applications Across Modalities: AI's application in medical imaging is not limited to a single type of scan; it spans various modalities, including X-rays for detecting conditions like pneumonia or bone fractures, MRIs for identifying tumours or neurological disorders, and CT scans for spotting abnormalities in the chest, abdomen, or other body parts. Each modality benefits from AI's ability to discern subtle details that may be overlooked by the human eye.

Enhanced Speed and Efficiency: AI algorithms can analyze medical images much faster than human radiologists, reducing the time from imaging to diagnosis. This speed is crucial in emergency situations or in conditions where early detection significantly improves prognosis, such as stroke or cancer.

IMPACT ON PATIENT OUTCOMES

Early Detection and Intervention: By improving the accuracy and speed of diagnoses, AI enables earlier detection of diseases, which is often key to successful treatment. Early intervention can lead to better management of chronic conditions, reduced complications, and, in many cases, curative treatments for diseases like cancer.

Reducing Diagnostic Errors: Diagnostic errors can have serious implications for patient care. AI helps minimize these errors by providing consistent, objective analysis. It serves as a valuable second opinion for radiologists, reducing the likelihood of misdiagnosis and ensuring patients receive the correct treatment promptly.

Personalized Treatment Plans: Beyond diagnosis, AI's ability to analyze and interpret complex medical data extends to predicting patient outcomes and recommending personalized treatment plans. By considering a patient's unique medical history, genetics, and disease characteristics, AI can suggest tailored treatment approaches that are more likely to be effective for the individual.

CHALLENGES AND CONSIDERATIONS

Data Privacy and Security: The use of sensitive medical images to train AI models raises concerns about data privacy and security. Ensuring that patient data is anonymized and protected is paramount.

Integration into Clinical Practice: Integrating AI tools into existing healthcare workflows without disrupting patient care or placing additional burdens on healthcare professionals is a challenge that requires careful planning and training.

Ethical and Regulatory Oversight: As AI takes on a more prominent role in diagnosis and treatment, ethical considerations and regulatory oversight become increasingly important to ensure these technologies are used safely and equitably.

CONCLUSION

AI's role in improving diagnostic accuracy through the analysis of medical images represents a significant advancement in healthcare. By enabling earlier detection of diseases, reducing diagnostic errors, and facilitating personalized treatment plans, AI has the potential to dramatically improve patient outcomes. However, realizing this potential fully requires addressing the technical, ethical, and practical challenges associated with integrating AI into healthcare systems.

ROLE OF AI IN DEVELOPING PERSONALIZED TREATMENT PLANS

The advent of Artificial Intelligence (AI) in healthcare has ushered in a new era of personalized medicine, where treatment plans are tailored to the individual characteristics of each patient. By leveraging vast amounts of patient data and advanced analytical capabilities, AI is transforming the way treatments are devised, promising more effective outcomes and a revolution in patient care. Let's explore the role of AI in developing personalized treatment plans, its methodologies, and its potential impact on healthcare.

ANALYZING PATIENT DATA

AI systems, particularly those based on machine learning algorithms, excel at analysing complex and multifaceted patient data. This includes genetic information, biomarkers, electronic health records (EHRs), imaging data, and even lifestyle factors. By sifting through this data, AI can identify patterns and correlations that may not be apparent to human clinicians.

Genomic Analysis: AI can analyze genetic data to identify mutations and variations that may influence how a patient responds to certain treatments. This is particularly relevant in oncology, where targeted therapies are selected based on the genetic makeup of a tumour.

Predictive Analytics: Machine learning models can predict disease progression and treatment responses by comparing a patient's data against historical outcomes from similar cases. This predictive capability is crucial for diseases with complex treatment pathways, such as cancer, diabetes, and cardiovascular diseases.

RECOMMENDING TAILORED TREATMENT APPROACHES

AI's ability to integrate and analyze diverse data sources enables it to recommend treatment approaches that are highly personalized. These recommendations are based on the likelihood of success, considering the patient's unique profile.

Treatment Optimization: For chronic conditions like diabetes, AI algorithms can recommend medication dosages and lifestyle interventions tailored to the patient's ongoing health data, optimizing treatment efficacy and minimizing side effects.

Clinical Decision Support Systems (CDSS): AI-powered CDSS provide healthcare professionals with evidence-based treatment recommendations. These systems consider the latest research, clinical guidelines, and patient-specific factors, aiding clinicians in making informed treatment decisions.

The predictive power of AI extends to forecasting treatment outcomes, enabling clinicians and patients to make more informed decisions about their care.

Outcome Prediction: By analysing data from similar patient profiles and treatment histories, AI can predict the potential outcomes of different treatment options. This helps in setting realistic expectations and in making decisions that align with the patient's preferences and values.

Risk Stratification: AI models can identify patients at high risk of adverse events or complications, allowing for pre-emptive adjustments to their treatment plans. This proactive approach can significantly improve patient safety and treatment success.

CHALLENGES AND ETHICAL CONSIDERATIONS

While the potential of AI in personalized medicine is vast, it also presents challenges and ethical considerations that must be addressed:

Data Privacy and Security: The use of sensitive personal health information raises concerns about data privacy and security. Ensuring that patient data is protected and used ethically is paramount.

Bias and Equity: AI models can perpetuate or amplify biases present in the training data. Ensuring that AI systems are trained on diverse datasets is crucial to avoid biased treatment recommendations and to promote equity in healthcare.

Clinical Integration: Integrating AI into clinical workflows in a way that complements the clinician's expertise and preserves the patient-clinician relationship is essential for the successful adoption of AI in personalized treatment planning.

CONCLUSION

AI's role in developing personalized treatment plans represents a significant leap forward in the pursuit of tailored healthcare. By analysing complex patient data to recommend customized treatment approaches and predict outcomes, AI has the potential to significantly enhance treatment efficacy and patient satisfaction. However, realizing this potential fully requires careful navigation of the associated challenges and ethical considerations, ensuring that AI serves as a valuable tool in the advancement of personalized medicine.

AI'S CONTRIBUTIONS TO MEDICAL RESEARCH

Artificial Intelligence (AI) is revolutionizing medical research, particularly in the realms of drug discovery and genomic analysis. By leveraging AI's computational power and advanced analytics, researchers can unravel complex biological processes, accelerate the identification of therapeutic compounds, and deepen our understanding of genetic factors in diseases. This transformative approach not only speeds up research but also enhances its precision, opening new avenues for treatment and prevention strategies.

AI IN DRUG DISCOVERY

The traditional drug discovery process is time-consuming and costly, often taking over a decade and billions of dollars to bring a new drug to market. AI is poised to dramatically streamline this process.

High-throughput Screening: AI algorithms can analyze vast libraries of chemical compounds quickly, predicting their potential as therapeutic agents. This high-throughput screening process identifies promising candidates for further testing, significantly reducing the time and resources required.

Predictive Modelling: AI models can predict how different compounds will interact with biological targets, helping to identify those with the highest therapeutic potential. These predictions are based on the compound's structure, known biological pathways, and data from previous studies, allowing researchers to focus on the most promising molecules.

Molecular Docking: AI is used in molecular docking simulations to predict how a drug molecule will bind to its target, such as a protein associated with a disease. This helps in designing drugs that can effectively modulate a biological target's activity, enhancing drug efficacy and reducing side effects.

AI IN GENOMIC ANALYSIS

Genomics, the study of an organism's complete set of DNA, including all of its genes, holds critical insights into the genetic factors underlying diseases. AI is significantly advancing genomic analysis, enabling personalized medicine approaches that tailor prevention and treatment to individual genetic profiles.

Genetic Variant Interpretation: AI algorithms can sift through genetic data from patients to identify mutations and variants associated with diseases. This capability is crucial for understanding the genetic basis of diseases and for developing targeted therapies.

Gene Expression Analysis: AI is used to analyze gene expression patterns, helping to identify which genes are active in disease states and how they interact. This information is vital for understanding disease mechanisms and for identifying potential targets for therapy.

Predictive Genomics: By analysing genetic data, AI can predict an individual's risk of developing certain diseases. This predictive power is essential for preventive medicine, allowing for early interventions that can delay or prevent the onset of disease.

ACCELERATING RESEARCH AND PERSONALIZED MEDICINE

The contributions of AI to drug discovery and genomic analysis are accelerating medical research and paving the way for personalized medicine, where treatments are tailored to the individual's genetic makeup.

Faster, More Efficient Research: AI's ability to quickly analyze and interpret vast amounts of data accelerates the pace of research, leading to faster identification of potential drugs and a deeper understanding of genetic factors in diseases.

Personalized Treatment Strategies: AI's insights into genetics and drug interactions enable the development of personalized treatment strategies that are more effective and have fewer side effects, improving patient outcomes.

CHALLENGES AND FUTURE DIRECTIONS

Despite its potential, the integration of AI into medical research faces challenges, including data privacy concerns, the need for large, annotated datasets for training AI models, and ensuring that AI systems are transparent and interpretable by researchers. Overcoming these challenges requires ongoing collaboration between computational scientists, biologists, and clinicians.

CONCLUSION

AI's contributions to drug discovery and genomic analysis are transforming medical research, making it faster, more precise, and increasingly personalized. As AI technologies continue to evolve, their potential to uncover new therapeutic compounds and unravel the genetic complexities of diseases promises to usher in a new era of medical breakthroughs and treatment strategies.

FRAUD DETECTION, TRADING, AND PERSONAL FINANCE

AI IN DETECTING AND PREVENTING FINANCIAL FRAUD

The financial sector has increasingly turned to Artificial Intelligence (AI) to bolster its defences against fraud, a pervasive issue costing billions annually. AI's ability to analyze vast datasets in real-time, recognize patterns, and predict fraudulent activities before they occur has made it an indispensable tool in the fight against financial crime. Here's how AI is transforming fraud detection and prevention:

MECHANISMS OF AI IN FRAUD DETECTION

Pattern Recognition: At the core of AI's fraud detection capabilities is its ability to recognize patterns and anomalies in data. Machine learning algorithms, trained on historical transaction data, learn to identify what constitutes normal transaction behaviour for an individual account or across the system. When a transaction deviates significantly from this established pattern, it can trigger an alert for potential fraud.

Anomaly Detection: AI systems are particularly adept at anomaly detection, which involves identifying outliers in datasets that do not conform to expected patterns. Unusual transactions, such as a high-value purchase in a foreign country or a sudden flurry of transactions in a short period, can be flagged for further investigation.

Predictive Analytics: Beyond recognizing existing patterns of fraud, AI can predict future fraudulent activities based on trends and correlations identified in the data. Predictive models can anticipate new types of fraud, allowing financial institutions to proactively update their defence mechanisms.

Natural Language Processing (NLP): NLP is used to monitor and analyze customer communication and public social media posts for potential signs of fraud. For example, discussions about exploiting security loopholes in a banking system could be detected by NLP algorithms, alerting the institution to potential threats.

Network Analysis: AI can analyze the relationships and networks between accounts to identify complex fraud schemes that might involve multiple parties and accounts. By understanding the network dynamics, AI can uncover sophisticated fraud rings that would be difficult for humans to detect.

IMPACT ON FINANCIAL INSTITUTIONS AND CUSTOMERS

Enhanced Security: AI-driven fraud detection systems significantly enhance the security of financial transactions, reducing the incidence of fraud and minimizing losses for both institutions and their customers.

Improved Customer Experience: By accurately distinguishing between legitimate and fraudulent transactions, AI reduces the occurrence of false positives—legitimate transactions mistakenly flagged as fraud. This improves the customer experience by avoiding unnecessary transaction declines and the associated inconvenience.

Adaptability to Emerging Threats: The financial fraud landscape is continuously evolving, with fraudsters constantly devising new schemes. AI's adaptability and learning capabilities ensure that fraud detection systems can evolve in tandem with emerging threats, providing enduring protection.

CHALLENGES AND CONSIDERATIONS

While AI dramatically improves fraud detection, it also presents challenges, including privacy concerns, the need for continuous data updates to train models, and the potential for AI systems to be manipulated by sophisticated fraudsters. Addressing these challenges requires a balanced approach that respects customer privacy, ensures data security, and maintains the integrity of AI systems.

CONCLUSION

AI's role in detecting and preventing financial fraud represents a significant advancement in securing financial transactions and protecting against losses. By leveraging AI's pattern recognition, anomaly detection, and predictive analytics capabilities, financial institutions can stay one step ahead of fraudsters, ensuring the safety and trust of their customers. As AI technology continues to evolve, its contributions to fraud detection are expected to become even more pronounced, further transforming the landscape of financial security.

IMPACT OF AI ON TRADING AND INVESTMENT STRATEGIES

The integration of Artificial Intelligence (AI) into the financial markets has significantly transformed trading and investment strategies. AI's ability to process vast amounts of data at unprecedented speeds has led to the development of sophisticated algorithmic trading systems and enhanced portfolio management techniques. This evolution is not only changing how trades are executed but also how investment portfolios are managed, offering both opportunities and challenges in the financial landscape.

AI IN ALGORITHMIC TRADING

Algorithmic trading, which involves the use of computer algorithms to execute trades at high speeds and volumes, has been revolutionized by AI. AI enhances these systems with predictive analytics, enabling them to make data-driven decisions in real-time.

High-Speed Decision Making: AI algorithms can analyze market data, news feeds, and financial reports in milliseconds, identifying patterns and trends that inform trading decisions. This speed allows for the exploitation of trading opportunities that would be impossible for human traders to identify or act upon in time.

Risk Management: AI systems can also assess the risk levels of different trading strategies in real-time, adjusting their approaches based on market volatility and other indicators to manage potential losses.

Market Efficiency: The widespread use of AI in algorithmic trading contributes to market efficiency by ensuring that prices reflect all available information. However, it also raises concerns about market stability, as AI-driven trades can amplify market movements, leading to increased volatility.

AI IN INVESTMENT PORTFOLIO MANAGEMENT

AI's role extends beyond trading to the management of investment portfolios, where it aids in asset allocation, risk assessment, and personalized investment solutions.

Asset Allocation: AI algorithms can process complex datasets to identify optimal asset allocation strategies, taking into account market conditions, economic indicators, and individual investor goals. This dynamic approach to portfolio management can adapt to changes in the market, potentially enhancing returns while managing risk.

Personalized Investment Solutions: AI enables the creation of personalized investment portfolios tailored to the specific risk tolerance, investment goals, and time horizons of individual investors. Robo-advisors, which use AI to offer investment advice and manage portfolios, exemplify this trend, providing cost-effective, personalized financial planning services.

Predictive Analytics for Long-Term Trends: AI models are employed to forecast long-term market trends and economic cycles, informing strategic investment decisions. By analysing historical data and current market signals, AI can provide insights into future market movements, aiding in the development of long-term investment strategies.

CHALLENGES AND ETHICAL CONSIDERATIONS

The use of AI in trading and investment strategies raises several challenges and ethical considerations:

Transparency and Accountability: The decision-making processes of AI systems can be opaque, making it difficult to understand how trading or investment decisions are made. This lack of transparency raises questions about accountability, especially in cases of financial loss or market disruption.

Regulatory Compliance: Ensuring that AI-driven trading and investment activities comply with existing financial regulations is crucial. Regulators are challenged to keep pace with technological advancements, necessitating updates to regulatory frameworks to address the unique aspects of AI in finance.

Market Fairness: The advantage that AI-driven systems provide to institutional investors could widen the gap between these entities and individual investors, raising concerns about market fairness and access.

CONCLUSION

AI's impact on trading and investment strategies represents a significant shift towards more automated, data-driven financial markets. While AI offers the promise of enhanced efficiency, improved risk management, and personalized investment solutions, it also presents challenges that need to be carefully managed. Balancing the benefits of AI with considerations of transparency, regulatory compliance, and market fairness will be crucial as the role of AI in finance continues to evolve.

HOW AI IS TRANSFORMING PERSONAL FINANCE MANAGEMENT

Artificial Intelligence (AI) is significantly transforming personal finance management, making it more accessible, efficient, and tailored to individual needs. Through AI-powered tools and applications, users can gain insights into their financial habits, receive personalized advice, and make more informed decisions about their savings, spending, and investments. This section explores various ways AI is reshaping personal finance management.

AI-POWERED CHATBOTS FOR FINANCIAL ADVICE

24/7 Accessibility: AI-powered chatbots provide users with round-the-clock financial advice, answering questions and offering guidance on a wide range of topics, from budgeting to investing. These chatbots can quickly access and analyze users' financial data, providing instant, personalized responses.

Financial Literacy: Beyond answering queries, these chatbots play a crucial role in enhancing financial literacy, explaining complex financial concepts in simple terms and offering tips to improve financial health.

ALGORITHMS FOR BUDGETING AND EXPENSE TRACKING

Automated Budgeting: AI algorithms analyze users' income, spending patterns, and financial goals to create personalized budgets. By categorizing expenses and identifying areas where users can cut back, these tools help individuals manage their finances more effectively.

Real-Time Expense Tracking: AI-driven applications automatically track and categorize expenses, providing users with real-time insights into their spending. This instant feedback helps users stay within their budget and make adjustments as needed.

PERSONALIZED SAVINGS AND INVESTMENT STRATEGIES

Optimizing Savings: AI tools analyze users' financial situations and goals to recommend optimal savings strategies. This might include suggesting changes to monthly savings amounts or advising on setting up emergency funds.

Tailored Investment Advice: Leveraging data on market trends and individual risk tolerance, AI can offer personalized investment advice. Robo-advisors, for example, use algorithms to manage users' investment portfolios, reallocating assets as market conditions change to optimize returns.

PREDICTIVE ANALYTICS FOR FINANCIAL PLANNING

Forecasting Financial Health: AI's predictive analytics capabilities enable it to forecast users' future financial health based on current trends in their income, spending, and saving habits. This foresight can prompt users to make proactive changes to avoid potential financial issues.

Debt Management: AI tools can also advise on managing and reducing debt, from suggesting payment strategies to negotiating better interest rates based on the user's credit history and financial behaviour.

CHALLENGES AND ETHICAL CONSIDERATIONS

While AI's role in personal finance management offers numerous benefits, it also raises challenges and ethical considerations:

Data Privacy and Security: The effectiveness of AI in personal finance relies on access to sensitive financial data. Ensuring the privacy and security of this data is paramount to protect users from potential breaches and misuse.

Bias and Fairness: AI systems must be carefully designed to avoid biases that could lead to unfair financial advice or discriminatory practices. This includes ensuring that algorithms do not inadvertently favour certain demographics over others.

Dependency: There's a risk that users might become overly dependent on AI for financial decisions, potentially undermining their ability to understand and manage their finances independently.

CONCLUSION

AI is revolutionizing personal finance management by providing tools that offer personalized advice, automate budgeting and expense tracking, and optimize savings and investment strategies. As these technologies continue to evolve, they promise to make financial management more intuitive and aligned with individual goals. However, addressing challenges related to data privacy, algorithmic bias, and user dependency will be crucial to fully realize the benefits of AI in personal finance.

AI IN MANUFACTURING AND SUPPLY CHAIN MANAGEMENT

The integration of Artificial Intelligence (AI) into manufacturing and supply chain management has been a game-changer, significantly enhancing efficiency, reducing costs, and improving product quality. By leveraging AI, companies can optimize manufacturing processes through predictive maintenance, quality control, and the design of more efficient production lines. Let's delve into these applications to understand how AI is transforming the manufacturing sector.

PREDICTIVE MAINTENANCE OF MACHINERY

Predictive Analytics for Equipment Maintenance: AI-driven predictive maintenance utilizes machine learning algorithms to analyze data from machinery sensors and predict potential failures before they occur. This approach allows manufacturers to perform maintenance only when needed, reducing downtime and maintenance costs.

Real-time Monitoring and Analysis: AI systems continuously monitor the condition of equipment, analysing data in real time to detect anomalies that may indicate impending failures. This proactive approach to maintenance helps prevent costly unplanned downtime and extends the lifespan of machinery.

QUALITY CONTROL USING COMPUTER VISION

Automated Inspection Systems: AI-powered computer vision systems are revolutionizing quality control in manufacturing. These systems can inspect products at high speeds with precision and accuracy far exceeding human capabilities. By analysing images of products on the production line, AI can identify defects, variations, and quality issues in real time.

Continuous Learning and Improvement: AI models used in quality control can learn from every inspection, continuously improving their ability to detect defects. This learning capability enables manufacturers to maintain high-quality standards and reduce waste.

DESIGNING MORE EFFICIENT PRODUCTION LINES

Optimization of Production Processes: AI algorithms can analyze production data to identify inefficiencies and bottlenecks in the manufacturing process. By simulating different scenarios and configurations, AI can recommend changes to the production line layout, machinery settings, and workflows that optimize efficiency and throughput.

Customization and Flexibility: AI enables more flexible production lines that can quickly adapt to changes in product design or demand. Machine learning algorithms can adjust machinery parameters in real time to accommodate different product variants, allowing manufacturers to offer greater customization without sacrificing efficiency.

IMPACT ON MANUFACTURING AND SUPPLY CHAIN MANAGEMENT

Enhanced Efficiency and Productivity: AI's ability to optimize manufacturing processes leads to significant improvements in efficiency and productivity. Manufacturers can produce more goods in less time while minimizing resource consumption.

Improved Product Quality: The application of AI in quality control ensures that products meet high-quality standards, enhancing customer satisfaction and reducing the cost associated with returns and repairs.

Supply Chain Optimization: Beyond manufacturing processes, AI plays a crucial role in supply chain management, optimizing inventory levels, forecasting demand, and improving logistics. This holistic approach to optimization ensures that manufacturing operations are aligned with supply chain dynamics, further enhancing efficiency and responsiveness.

CONCLUSION

AI's applications in optimizing manufacturing processes represent a significant leap forward for the industry. From predictive maintenance and quality control to the design of efficient production lines, AI is enabling manufacturers to achieve new levels of efficiency, quality, and flexibility. As AI technology continues to evolve, its role in manufacturing and supply chain management is set to become even more pivotal, driving innovation and competitiveness in the sector.

THE ROLE OF AI IN SUPPLY CHAIN MANAGEMENT

Artificial Intelligence (AI) is revolutionizing supply chain management by offering unprecedented capabilities for forecasting demand, optimizing inventory, and enhancing logistics operations. These advancements are enabling companies to respond more swiftly and efficiently to market changes, reduce operational costs, and improve customer satisfaction. Let's delve into the specifics of how AI is transforming supply chain management.

AI IN DEMAND FORECASTING

Advanced Predictive Analytics: AI leverages machine learning algorithms to analyze historical sales data, market trends, consumer behaviour, and external factors such as economic indicators and weather patterns. This comprehensive analysis allows for highly accurate demand forecasting, enabling companies to anticipate market needs more precisely.

Real-time Adjustments: AI systems can continuously update demand forecasts in real-time based on new data, ensuring that predictions remain accurate even as market conditions change. This agility allows companies to be more responsive to unexpected shifts in demand, reducing the risk of stockouts or excess inventory.

OPTIMIZING INVENTORY LEVELS

Automated Inventory Management: AI algorithms optimize inventory levels by determining the optimal stock quantities for each product, considering factors like lead times, demand variability, and storage costs. This optimization helps maintain the balance between minimizing inventory costs and meeting customer demand without delays.

Dynamic Replenishment: AI-driven systems can automate the replenishment process, ordering new stock just in time to replenish inventory without overstocking. This dynamic approach reduces inventory holding costs and minimizes the risk of obsolescence.

ENHANCING LOGISTICS AND ROUTE OPTIMIZATION

Route Optimization: AI algorithms analyze various factors, including traffic patterns, weather conditions, and delivery windows, to determine the most efficient delivery routes. This optimization reduces fuel consumption and delivery times, enhancing operational efficiency and customer satisfaction.

Autonomous Vehicles in Logistics: AI is at the forefront of developing autonomous vehicles for logistics, promising to transform delivery operations. Autonomous trucks and drones can optimize routes in real-time, reduce human error, and operate around the clock, further improving the efficiency and reliability of delivery services.

SUPPLY CHAIN RESILIENCE AND SUSTAINABILITY

Building Resilient Supply Chains: AI enhances supply chain resilience by providing tools for risk assessment and mitigation strategies. By analysing data on suppliers, geopolitical risks, and global market trends, AI can help identify potential disruptions and suggest actions to mitigate these risks.

Sustainability: AI contributes to more sustainable supply chain practices by optimizing routes and inventory levels to reduce waste and emissions. Predictive maintenance for vehicles and machinery, enabled by AI, also contributes to sustainability by ensuring that equipment operates efficiently and with minimal environmental impact.

CHALLENGES AND FUTURE DIRECTIONS

While AI offers transformative potential for supply chain management, challenges remain, including data privacy concerns, the need for significant investments in technology and infrastructure, and the requirement for skilled personnel to manage and interpret AI systems. Overcoming these challenges will be crucial for companies looking to fully leverage AI in their supply chain operations.

CONCLUSION

AI's role in supply chain management is profound, offering innovative solutions for demand forecasting, inventory optimization, and logistics. As companies continue to embrace AI technologies, the future of supply chain management looks set to be more efficient, responsive, and sustainable. The ongoing development and integration of AI into supply chain practices promise to further enhance these benefits, driving operational excellence and competitive advantage in an increasingly complex global market.

THE FUTURE POTENTIAL OF AI IN SMART FACTORIES

The concept of fully automated, smart factories represents the pinnacle of manufacturing evolution, where Artificial Intelligence (AI) orchestrates all aspects of production, from supply chain management to the manufacturing floor, maintenance, and quality control. This vision of Industry 4.0 promises unprecedented efficiency, flexibility, and customization capabilities. However, realizing this potential comes with significant challenges, especially when integrating AI into traditional manufacturing environments.

ADVANCEMENTS TOWARDS FULLY AUTOMATED FACTORIES

Seamless Integration Across Operations: AI enables the seamless integration of various manufacturing processes, allowing for real-time communication and coordination across different stages of production. This integration can lead to significant improvements in efficiency and reduce waste by precisely aligning supply with demand.

Predictive Maintenance and Quality Control: Through the use of sensors and AI analytics, smart factories can predict when machines are likely to fail or when a process is deviating from quality standards. This predictive capability allows for proactive maintenance and quality control, minimizing downtime and ensuring consistent product quality.

Customization at Scale: AI-driven manufacturing processes enable mass customization, allowing factories to produce goods tailored to individual customer preferences without sacrificing efficiency or significantly increasing costs.

CHALLENGES IN INTEGRATING AI INTO TRADITIONAL MANUFACTURING

WORKFORCE IMPLICATIONS

Job Displacement and Transformation: The shift towards fully automated factories may lead to job displacement, particularly for roles that are highly repetitive and can be easily automated. However, it also creates opportunities for new roles focused on managing and maintaining AI systems, data analysis, and strategic decision-making.

Skill Gap: There is a growing need for a workforce skilled in AI, robotics, data analytics, and digital technologies. Traditional manufacturing workers may require retraining or upskilling to fit into the new manufacturing paradigm, posing challenges in workforce development and transition strategies.

TECHNICAL AND OPERATIONAL CHALLENGES

Integration with Existing Systems: Many manufacturing environments operate on legacy systems that may not be readily compatible with the latest AI technologies. Upgrading these systems or ensuring seamless integration with new AI solutions can be complex and costly.

Data Privacy and Security: The reliance on data for AI-driven manufacturing increases the risk of data breaches and cyber-attacks. Ensuring the privacy and security of sensitive information is paramount, requiring robust cybersecurity measures.

Reliability and Trust: Building trust in AI systems' decisions, especially in critical processes where errors can have significant consequences, is essential. Ensuring the reliability and explain ability of AI decisions remains a challenge.

FUTURE DIRECTIONS AND OPPORTUNITIES

Collaborative AI and Human Workforce: Developing AI systems that complement and augment human capabilities, rather than replace them, can lead to more effective and resilient manufacturing environments. Collaborative robots (cobots) working alongside humans are an example of this approach.

Continuous Learning and Improvement: Implementing AI systems that can learn and adapt over time will be crucial for addressing the dynamic nature of manufacturing needs and market demands. This continuous improvement can drive innovation and maintain competitiveness.

Ethical and Sustainable Manufacturing: AI offers the potential to make manufacturing more sustainable by optimizing resource use and reducing waste. Ethically deploying AI, with consideration for its societal impacts, will be key to achieving sustainable and responsible manufacturing practices.

CONCLUSION

The journey towards fully automated, smart factories is fraught with challenges but also brimming with potential. By addressing workforce implications, integrating AI into existing systems, and ensuring the ethical use of technology, the manufacturing sector can unlock the full benefits of AI. This transition not only promises to revolutionize how goods are produced but also how the workforce is shaped and how businesses compete on a global scale.

CHAPTER 8: ETHICAL CONSIDERATIONS AND SOCIAL IMPACTS

BIAS AND FAIRNESS IN AI SYSTEMS

The integration of Artificial Intelligence (AI) into various facets of daily life has underscored the critical issue of bias within these systems. Bias in AI can lead to unfair, discriminatory outcomes that disproportionately affect marginalized groups, raising significant ethical concerns. Understanding the origins of this bias, including the role of biased datasets and the lack of diversity among AI developers, is crucial for developing more equitable AI applications.

ORIGINS OF BIAS IN AI SYSTEMS

Biased Datasets: AI systems learn to make decisions based on data. If this data is biased, the AI's decisions will likely perpetuate or even exacerbate these biases. For example, if an AI system trained to automate resume screening for job applications is fed historical hiring data that reflects gender or racial biases, it may learn to favour certain demographics over others, despite qualifications.

Lack of Diversity Among AI Developers: The teams developing AI systems often lack diversity in terms of gender, race, ethnicity, and socio-economic background. This lack of diversity can lead to blind spots, where developers might not recognize or anticipate how different groups could be adversely affected by an AI system. For instance, facial recognition technologies have been shown to have higher error rates for women and people of colour, partly because the datasets used for training these systems did not include a diverse range of faces.

CONTRIBUTING FACTORS TO UNFAIR OUTCOMES

Reflecting Societal Biases: AI systems can inadvertently learn and perpetuate societal biases present in the data they are trained on. These biases can manifest in various applications, from predictive policing tools that disproportionately target minority communities to credit scoring algorithms that disadvantage certain groups.

Amplification of Bias: AI can not only reflect but also amplify biases. For example, recommendation algorithms on social media platforms can create echo chambers that reinforce users' pre-existing beliefs, potentially deepening societal divisions.

Opaque Decision-Making Processes: Many AI systems operate as "black boxes," where the decision-making process is not transparent. This opacity can make it difficult to identify and correct biases, leading to unfair outcomes that cannot be easily traced back to their source.

STRATEGIES FOR MITIGATING BIAS

Diversifying Training Data: Ensuring that the datasets used to train AI systems are diverse and representative of all groups can help reduce bias. This includes not only diversifying the data but also carefully annotating it to identify potential biases.

Increasing Diversity Among Developers: Building more diverse teams of AI developers can help identify potential biases and fairness issues early in the development process. Diverse perspectives can lead to more inclusive design choices and consideration of a wider range of ethical implications.

Developing Bias Detection and Correction Methodologies: Implementing tools and methodologies for detecting and correcting bias in AI systems is essential. This can involve regular audits of AI systems for biased outcomes and the development of algorithms specifically designed to identify and mitigate bias.

Implementing Transparent AI Systems: Increasing the transparency of AI decision-making processes can help identify and address biases. This includes developing explainable AI models that allow users and regulators to understand how decisions are made.

CONCLUSION

The origins of bias in AI systems are multifaceted, stemming from biased datasets, the lack of diversity among developers, and broader societal biases. Addressing these issues requires a concerted effort to diversify data and development teams, develop robust methodologies for detecting and correcting bias, and enhance the transparency of AI systems. By tackling these challenges, we can work towards more equitable and fair AI applications that serve the needs of all segments of society.

THE IMPACT OF BIASED AI ON SOCIETY

The impact of biased Artificial Intelligence (AI) systems on society is profound, particularly in areas where decisions significantly affect individuals' lives and livelihoods, such as criminal justice, hiring practices, and financial services. The consequences of such biases disproportionately affect marginalized communities, exacerbating existing inequalities and perpetuating systemic discrimination. Understanding these impacts is crucial for developing strategies to mitigate bias and ensure AI technologies are used ethically and equitably.

IMPACT ON CRIMINAL JUSTICE

Risk Assessment Tools: AI-driven risk assessment tools are increasingly used in criminal justice to inform decisions on bail, sentencing, and parole. However, studies have shown that some of these tools can exhibit racial biases, overestimating the risk of recidivism for Black defendants compared to White defendants. This can lead to harsher sentences and a higher likelihood of being denied bail for marginalized individuals, perpetuating racial disparities within the criminal justice system.

Facial Recognition: AI-powered facial recognition technologies used by law enforcement have been found to have higher error rates for people of colour, women, and the elderly. Misidentification can lead to wrongful arrests and surveillance, disproportionately affecting marginalized communities and eroding trust in law enforcement.

IMPACT ON HIRING PRACTICES

Automated Resume Screening: AI systems used to screen job applications can inherit biases from historical hiring data or biased criteria, leading to the exclusion of qualified candidates from underrepresented groups. For example, if a system is trained on data from a company where leadership positions have historically been held by men, the AI might undervalue resumes from women or non-binary individuals, perpetuating gender disparities in employment.

Video Interview Analysis: AI tools that analyze video interviews to assess candidates' suitability can also exhibit biases, particularly if they rely on problematic criteria such as speech patterns, facial expressions, or even the background visible in the video. These systems may unfairly disadvantage candidates from different cultural backgrounds or those with disabilities.

IMPACT ON FINANCIAL SERVICES

Credit Scoring: AI models used for credit scoring can incorporate biases that result in lower credit scores for individuals from certain racial or ethnic groups, even when controlling for financial behaviours. This can limit access to loans, mortgages, and other financial services, reinforcing economic disparities.

Insurance Premiums: AI algorithms that determine insurance premiums and coverage can also reflect biases, potentially leading to higher premiums for marginalized communities based on discriminatory criteria, further entrenching socio-economic divides.

CONSEQUENCES FOR MARGINALIZED COMMUNITIES

The consequences of biased AI systems extend beyond individual injustices, contributing to systemic inequality and hindering social mobility for marginalized communities. By reinforcing existing biases, these systems can close off opportunities for employment, fair treatment in the criminal justice system, and access to financial services, perpetuating cycles of disadvantage.

ADDRESSING THE IMPACT

Mitigating the impact of biased AI on society requires a multifaceted approach:

Transparency and Accountability: Implementing mechanisms for transparency in AI decision-making processes and establishing clear lines of accountability for biased outcomes.

Diverse Data and Development Teams: Ensuring diversity in both the data used to train AI systems and the teams developing them to reduce the risk of biases being encoded into AI models.

Regulatory Oversight: Developing and enforcing regulations that require regular auditing of AI systems for bias and mandating corrective measures when biases are identified.

Community Engagement: Involving marginalized communities in the development and oversight of AI systems to ensure their needs and perspectives are considered.

CONCLUSION

The impact of biased AI on society, particularly in critical areas like criminal justice, hiring practices, and financial services, highlights the urgent need for concerted efforts to address AI bias. By acknowledging and tackling these challenges, we can harness the potential of AI technologies to contribute positively to society, ensuring they serve to bridge rather than widen social divides.

STRATEGIES FOR MITIGATING BIAS IN AI

Mitigating bias in Artificial Intelligence (AI) is crucial for ensuring that AI systems are fair, ethical, and beneficial for all segments of society. Addressing AI bias involves a multifaceted approach that encompasses diversifying AI development teams, enhancing bias detection and correction methodologies, and fostering transparency and accountability in AI systems. Here's a closer look at these strategies and how they can be implemented to combat bias in AI.

DIVERSIFYING AI TEAMS

Inclusive Recruitment: Actively recruiting and supporting individuals from diverse backgrounds, including different races, genders, ethnicities, and socio-economic statuses, can bring varied perspectives to AI development. This diversity helps in identifying potential biases that might not be apparent to a more homogenous group.

Fostering an Inclusive Culture: Beyond recruitment, creating an inclusive culture that values diverse perspectives and encourages their expression is essential. This includes providing training on unconscious bias and creating channels for team members to voice concerns about potential biases in AI projects.

DEVELOPING BIAS DETECTION AND CORRECTION METHODOLOGIES

Bias Audits: Regularly conducting bias audits on AI systems can help identify and quantify biases. These audits can be performed by internal teams or independent third parties to assess how AI decisions may vary across different demographic groups.

Algorithmic Fairness Approaches: Implementing algorithmic fairness approaches, such as fairness through unawareness, equality of opportunity, or demographic parity, depending on the context of the AI application. These approaches require developers to define what fairness means in the context of their specific AI system and adjust the algorithm accordingly.

Continuous Monitoring and Updating: AI systems should be continuously monitored for biased outcomes, even after deployment. Machine learning models can drift over time as they encounter new data, necessitating regular updates and adjustments to maintain fairness.

IMPLEMENTING TRANSPARENT AI SYSTEMS

Explainable AI (XAI): Developing AI systems that are explainable and interpretable helps stakeholders understand how decisions are made. This transparency is crucial for identifying when and why biased decisions occur, allowing for targeted interventions.

Documentation and Reporting: Maintaining comprehensive documentation of data sources, model decisions, and the rationale behind algorithmic choices can aid in accountability. Regular reporting on AI performance, including assessments of fairness and bias, should be standard practice.

Regulatory Compliance and Standards: Adhering to emerging regulations and standards focused on AI ethics and fairness, such as the EU's AI Act or the Algorithmic Accountability Act in the U.S., can guide organizations in implementing best practices for bias mitigation.

ENGAGING WITH AFFECTED COMMUNITIES

Stakeholder Engagement: Engaging with communities and stakeholders affected by AI decisions can provide insights into the real-world impacts of AI bias. This engagement can inform more empathetic and equitable AI development practices.

Public Oversight: Establishing mechanisms for public oversight of AI systems, including avenues for reporting biased outcomes and participating in the review of AI impacts, can enhance accountability and trust in AI technologies.

CONCLUSION

Mitigating bias in AI is an ongoing challenge that requires commitment, vigilance, and a proactive approach from all stakeholders involved in AI development and deployment. By diversifying AI teams, enhancing bias detection and correction methodologies, and fostering transparency and accountability, we can make significant strides toward more equitable and fair AI systems. These efforts not only contribute to the ethical use of AI but also enhance the technology's societal acceptance and effectiveness.

PRIVACY CONCERNS AND DATA SECURITY

The advent of Artificial Intelligence (AI) and its reliance on large datasets for training and operation has significantly heightened concerns around privacy and data security. The collection and analysis of vast amounts of personal information by AI systems pose several risks, including the potential misuse of data and the threat of pervasive surveillance. Understanding these risks is crucial for developing strategies to protect individual privacy in the age of AI.

PRIVACY RISKS IN AI DATA COLLECTION AND ANALYSIS

Massive Data Collection: AI systems often require extensive datasets to learn and make accurate predictions. This necessity leads to the collection of vast amounts of personal information, ranging from online behaviour and location data to personal communications and biometric data. The sheer volume of data collected poses inherent risks to individual privacy, as it may contain sensitive information that individuals may not wish to be collected or analysed.

Invasive Profiling: AI's capability to analyze and cross-reference data can lead to the creation of detailed profiles of individuals. These profiles can reveal personal preferences, behaviours, and even predict future actions. While profiling can be used for benign purposes, such as personalizing services, it also has the potential for misuse, including targeted manipulation or discrimination.

Potential for Surveillance: The use of AI in public and private surveillance systems has raised significant concerns about the erosion of privacy and the potential for constant monitoring. AI-enhanced surveillance can track individuals' movements, analyze facial expressions, and even predict behaviour, leading to a society where individuals may feel they are constantly being watched and evaluated.

DATA SECURITY CONCERNS

Vulnerability to Data Breaches: The large datasets used by AI systems are attractive targets for cyberattacks. A data breach involving AI systems can lead to the exposure of sensitive personal information on a massive scale, with severe consequences for the individuals affected.

AI Exploitation: AI systems themselves can be exploited by malicious actors. For example, attackers could use adversarial attacks to trick AI systems into making incorrect decisions or revealing sensitive information, further compromising data security.

Data Minimization and Anonymization: Employing data minimization strategies, where only the necessary data is collected, and anonymizing data to remove personally identifiable information can help reduce privacy risks.

Robust Data Security Measures: Implementing state-of-the-art data security measures, including encryption, access controls, and regular security audits, is essential for protecting datasets from unauthorized access and breaches.

Transparency and Consent: Ensuring transparency in how AI systems collect, use, and analyze data, and obtaining explicit consent from individuals, can help mitigate privacy concerns. Individuals should have the right to know what data is being collected about them and for what purposes.

Regulatory Compliance: Adhering to privacy regulations, such as the General Data Protection Regulation (GDPR) in the European Union, which sets strict guidelines for data collection, processing, and storage, is crucial for protecting individual privacy.

Ethical AI Development: Embedding ethical considerations into the development and deployment of AI systems, including respect for privacy and the implementation of ethical guidelines, can help address privacy and data security concerns.

CONCLUSION

The privacy risks and data security concerns associated with AI's collection and analysis of large datasets are significant, touching on issues of personal autonomy, freedom, and the potential for misuse. Addressing these concerns requires a multifaceted approach that includes technical measures, ethical AI development practices, regulatory compliance, and a commitment to respecting individual privacy rights. By taking these steps, we can harness the benefits of AI while safeguarding privacy and data security.

THE CHALLENGES OF ENSURING DATA SECURITY IN AI SYSTEMS

Ensuring data security in Artificial Intelligence (AI) systems presents unique challenges that stem from the inherent characteristics of AI technologies and their integration into digital infrastructures. The vulnerabilities introduced by AI not only pose risks to personal data security but also have broader implications for national security. Understanding these challenges is crucial for developing robust security measures that can protect against potential threats.

VULNERABILITIES INTRODUCED BY AI

Attack Surfaces in Machine Learning Models: AI systems, particularly those based on machine learning, can introduce new attack surfaces. For instance, adversarial attacks involve manipulating the input data to AI models in subtle ways that lead to incorrect outputs. These vulnerabilities can be exploited to bypass security systems, manipulate automated decision-making processes, or cause AI systems to reveal sensitive information.

Data Poisoning: Data poisoning attacks target the training data used by machine learning models, inserting false or malicious data that can skew the model's learning process and compromise its integrity. This can lead to flawed decision-making or vulnerabilities that attackers can exploit once the model is deployed.

Model Stealing and Reverse Engineering: AI models, especially those deployed in competitive commercial environments, are valuable intellectual property. Attackers may attempt to steal or reverse-engineer machine learning models to uncover proprietary information, replicate the models for unauthorized use, or identify weaknesses in the models that can be exploited.

IMPLICATIONS FOR PERSONAL AND NATIONAL SECURITY

Personal Data Security: The vulnerabilities in AI systems can lead to significant risks for personal data security. For example, adversarial attacks on biometric identification systems can result in unauthorized access to personal accounts or secure facilities. Similarly, data poisoning can compromise the integrity of personal data used for various services, leading to incorrect or harmful outcomes.

National Security Concerns: AI technologies are increasingly integrated into critical infrastructure and national defence systems. Vulnerabilities in these AI systems can be exploited by adversaries to disrupt essential services, compromise military operations, or gain access to sensitive government data. The potential for AI to be used in autonomous weapons systems also raises concerns about the security and reliability of AI decision-making in conflict situations.

STRATEGIES FOR ENHANCING DATA SECURITY IN AI SYSTEMS

Robust Model Training and Validation: Implementing rigorous training and validation processes for AI models can help identify vulnerabilities and ensure the integrity of the models. This includes using diverse and secure datasets for training and regularly testing models against potential adversarial attacks.

Continuous Monitoring and Updating: AI systems should be continuously monitored for signs of security breaches or attempts to manipulate model outputs. Regular updates and patches can address newly discovered vulnerabilities, ensuring that AI systems remain secure over time.

Secure Data Practices: Employing secure data practices, such as encryption of data both at rest and in transit, can protect against unauthorized access to the data used by AI systems. Access controls and audit logs can also help track data usage and identify potential security breaches.

Collaboration and Information Sharing: Collaboration between industry, academia, and government agencies can facilitate the sharing of information about AI vulnerabilities and threats. Joint efforts can lead to the development of standardized security protocols and best practices for AI systems.

CONCLUSION

The integration of AI into digital infrastructures introduces complex challenges for data security, with significant implications for both personal and national security. Addressing these challenges requires a comprehensive approach that includes robust model training, continuous monitoring, secure data practices, and collaboration across sectors. By acknowledging and actively addressing the vulnerabilities introduced by AI, we can leverage the benefits of AI technologies while safeguarding against potential threats.

BEST PRACTICES FOR PROTECTING PRIVACY AND ENSURING DATA SECURITY

The rapid advancement and deployment of Artificial Intelligence (AI) technologies necessitate stringent measures to protect privacy and ensure data security. Best practices and regulatory frameworks play a crucial role in establishing standards and guidelines for ethical AI development and deployment. These measures are essential for maintaining public trust in AI technologies and safeguarding individuals' rights. Here's an outline of the key practices and regulatory frameworks that contribute to privacy protection and data security in AI.

ENCRYPTION

Data Encryption: Encrypting data at rest and in transit is fundamental to protecting it from unauthorized access. Encryption should be applied to both the datasets used to train AI models and the data processed by deployed AI systems.

Model Encryption: Encrypting AI models themselves can protect proprietary information and prevent tampering, ensuring that the models operate as intended without being compromised.

ANONYMIZATION AND DATA MINIMIZATION

Anonymizing Data: Removing personally identifiable information from datasets used in AI development helps mitigate privacy risks. Techniques such as differential privacy can be employed to anonymize data in a way that preserves its utility for training AI models while protecting individual privacy.

Data Minimization: Collecting only the data necessary for a specific AI application reduces exposure to privacy risks. This practice aligns with the principle of data minimization, emphasizing efficiency and privacy protection.

REGULAR AUDITS AND RISK ASSESSMENTS

Conducting Privacy Impact Assessments: Regular privacy impact assessments can identify potential risks to personal data privacy arising from AI applications. These assessments should inform the development process, guiding the implementation of mitigating measures.

Security Audits: Regular security audits of AI systems, including penetration testing and vulnerability scanning, can identify and rectify security weaknesses, protecting against data breaches and unauthorized access.

REGULATORY FRAMEWORKS FOR AI

GENERAL DATA PROTECTION REGULATION (GDPR)

GDPR Compliance: The GDPR sets a high standard for data protection and privacy for individuals within the European Union. It emphasizes principles such as data protection by design and by default, the right to explanation for automated decisions, and strict consent requirements for data processing.

Rights of Data Subjects: The GDPR grants individuals rights over their data, including the right to access, rectify, and erase their data. AI developers must ensure their systems comply with these rights, particularly when AI is used in decision-making processes that affect individuals.

OTHER RELEVANT LEGISLATION AND FRAMEWORKS

California Consumer Privacy Act (CCPA): Similar to the GDPR, the CCPA provides consumers with rights over their personal information, including the right to know about data collection and the right to opt-out of the sale of their personal information.

AI-specific Regulations: Various jurisdictions are considering or have introduced AI-specific regulations that address ethical considerations, transparency, and accountability in AI systems. The European Union's proposed Artificial Intelligence Act is an example of comprehensive legislation aimed at regulating AI applications based on their risk levels.

THE ROLE OF INTERNATIONAL STANDARDS

ISO/IEC Standards: International standards, such as those developed by the International Organization for Standardization (ISO) and the International Electrotechnical Commission (IEC), provide guidelines for data protection and cybersecurity in AI systems. Adhering to these standards can help organizations implement effective privacy and security measures.

CONCLUSION

Protecting privacy and ensuring data security in AI requires a combination of robust technical measures, adherence to best practices, and compliance with regulatory frameworks. Encryption, anonymization, data minimization, regular audits, and risk assessments are key practices that, alongside regulations like the GDPR and CCPA, form the foundation for ethical AI development and deployment. As AI technologies continue to evolve, so too will the strategies and regulations designed to safeguard privacy and security, necessitating ongoing vigilance and adaptation by all stakeholders involved.

OPPORTUNITIES AND CHALLENGES

The advent of Artificial Intelligence (AI) is reshaping the landscape of employment, presenting both significant opportunities and challenges. While concerns about AI leading to job displacement persist, there is also considerable potential for AI to create new job opportunities and industries, particularly in areas ripe for growth and innovation. This analysis explores how AI is expected to drive employment trends and the sectors most likely to benefit from its transformative impact.

AI-DRIVEN GROWTH AND INNOVATION

Healthcare: AI is poised to revolutionize healthcare, not only by improving diagnostic accuracy and patient care but also by creating demand for new roles. These include AI healthcare technicians, who ensure the proper functioning of AI diagnostic tools, and data privacy specialists focused on protecting patient information. Additionally, personalized medicine, powered by AI's data analysis capabilities, could lead to roles in genetic counselling and tailored treatment planning.

Cybersecurity: As cyber threats become more sophisticated, the demand for AI-enhanced cybersecurity solutions is growing. This trend is expected to create jobs for AI security analysts who can work alongside intelligent systems to identify and neutralize threats more efficiently than ever before. The development of AI-driven security tools will also require skilled programmers and engineers dedicated to building resilient digital defences.

Sustainable Energy: AI's ability to optimize energy consumption and integrate renewable energy sources into the grid is transforming the energy sector. New job opportunities are emerging for AI specialists focused on improving energy efficiency, managing smart grids, and developing predictive maintenance schedules for renewable energy installations.

Agriculture: AI is introducing innovative solutions to increase agricultural productivity and sustainability. Roles in this sector may include AI agronomists who use data analysis to improve crop yields and sustainability consultants who leverage AI to develop environmentally friendly farming practices. Additionally, the development of autonomous farming equipment is creating jobs in robotics and machine learning engineering.

Creative Industries: AI is not only automating aspects of content creation but also enabling new forms of artistic expression. This opens up opportunities for creative professionals who can blend AI tools with human creativity to produce unique artworks, films, and music. Furthermore, the demand for AI-generated content is fostering new roles in content curation and quality assurance.

NAVIGATING THE CHALLENGES

While AI offers substantial opportunities for job creation, the transition may not be seamless. Challenges include:

Skills Gap: The demand for AI-related skills is outpacing the current supply of qualified workers. Addressing this gap requires significant investments in education and training programs to equip the workforce with the necessary technical skills.

Job Displacement: Certain sectors, particularly those involving routine tasks, are at risk of significant job displacement due to AI automation. Mitigating this impact involves retraining programs and policies that support workers in transitioning to new roles.

Ethical Considerations: The development and deployment of AI must be guided by ethical considerations to ensure that the benefits of AI-driven employment growth are equitably distributed. This includes addressing biases in AI algorithms that could lead to discriminatory hiring practices.

CONCLUSION

The potential of AI to create new job opportunities and industries is significant, with areas such as healthcare, cybersecurity, sustainable energy, agriculture, and creative industries poised for growth and innovation. However, realizing this potential requires proactive measures to address the challenges of job displacement, the skills gap, and ethical considerations. By navigating these challenges effectively, society can harness the transformative power of AI to foster employment growth and drive innovation across diverse sectors.

CHALLENGES POSED BY AI TO EMPLOYMENT

The integration of Artificial Intelligence (AI) into various sectors is transforming the landscape of employment, presenting challenges that need to be carefully managed to harness AI's full potential while mitigating its adverse effects. Two primary concerns are job displacement due to automation and the emergence of a skills gap as the labour market evolves to meet the demands of an AI-driven economy.

JOB DISPLACEMENT DUE TO AUTOMATION

Routine and Manual Jobs: AI and automation technologies are particularly adept at performing routine, repetitive tasks more efficiently than human workers. This capability poses a significant risk of job displacement in sectors reliant on manual labour and routine cognitive tasks, such as manufacturing, transportation, and administrative roles. The concern is that machines could replace human labour in these areas, leading to widespread unemployment among workers with skill sets tailored to these jobs.

Economic and Social Implications: The displacement of jobs due to AI-driven automation has broader economic and social implications. It could lead to increased income inequality, as the economic benefits of AI are disproportionately accrued by those with the capital to invest in and deploy these technologies. Additionally, there could be significant social challenges, including the erosion of community structures and increased mental health issues among displaced workers.

THE SKILLS GAP IN AN AI-DRIVEN ECONOMY

Evolving Skill Requirements: As AI technologies become more integrated into the workplace, the skill sets required for employment are evolving. There is a growing demand for workers with expertise in AI, machine learning, data analysis, and related technical skills. However, there is currently a mismatch between these emerging skill requirements and the existing capabilities of much of the workforce, leading to a skills gap.

Education and Training Challenges: Addressing the skills gap requires significant changes to education and training programs to prepare new entrants to the workforce and re-skill existing workers. This includes not only technical training in AI and related fields but also education in soft skills such as critical thinking, creativity, and emotional intelligence, which are less susceptible to automation.

Access and Equity Issues: The need for re-skilling and up-skilling presents access and equity challenges. Workers from disadvantaged backgrounds may have fewer opportunities to engage in lifelong learning or access new training programs. Without targeted interventions, the skills gap could exacerbate existing inequalities in the labour market.

STRATEGIES FOR ADDRESSING EMPLOYMENT CHALLENGES

Policy Interventions: Governments and policymakers play a crucial role in mitigating the impact of AI on employment. This could include implementing policies that encourage the creation of new jobs in sectors likely to expand due to AI, such as technology, healthcare, and renewable energy.

Support for Displaced Workers: Programs that support workers displaced by AI and automation are essential. This could involve unemployment benefits, retraining programs, and services that help workers transition into new roles in emerging sectors.

Public-Private Partnerships: Collaboration between the public sector, private industry, and educational institutions can help address the skills gap. Initiatives could include apprenticeships, vocational training programs, and partnerships with universities to align curricula with the needs of an AI-driven economy.

CONCLUSION

The challenges posed by AI to employment, including job displacement and the skills gap, require a coordinated response from governments, businesses, and educational institutions. By proactively addressing these challenges, it is possible to mitigate the adverse effects of AI on the workforce and leverage the technology to create new opportunities for employment and economic growth. Ensuring that the benefits of AI are broadly shared across society will be key to navigating the transition to an AI-driven economy.

STRATEGIES FOR NAVIGATING THE EMPLOYMENT IMPACTS OF AI

Navigating the employment impacts of Artificial Intelligence (AI) requires a multifaceted approach that combines education and retraining programs, policy interventions, and the strengthening of social safety nets. These strategies aim to mitigate the challenges posed by AI, such as job displacement and the skills gap, ensuring that the workforce can adapt to and thrive in an AI-driven economy. Here's an exploration of these strategies:

EDUCATION AND RETRAINING PROGRAMS

Lifelong Learning: Promote the concept of lifelong learning to ensure that workers can continuously update their skills in response to technological advancements. This includes access to online courses, workshops, and certification programs in AI, data science, and other relevant fields.

Vocational Training and Apprenticeships: Expand vocational training and apprenticeship programs to prepare individuals for jobs in sectors where AI creates new opportunities, such as healthcare, cybersecurity, and renewable energy. These programs should focus on both technical skills and soft skills like problem-solving and teamwork, which are crucial in the AI era.

Partnerships with Educational Institutions: Encourage partnerships between businesses, governments, and educational institutions to align curricula with the evolving needs of the labour market. This collaboration can help ensure that education programs provide students with the skills necessary for success in an AI-driven economy.

POLICY INTERVENTIONS TO SUPPORT DISPLACED WORKERS

Job Transition Programs: Implement programs that assist workers displaced by AI in transitioning to new roles. This could include career counselling, job matching services, and financial support during the transition period.

Incentives for Reskilling: Offer incentives to both individuals and companies for investing in retraining. For individuals, this could take the form of tax credits or subsidies for educational programs. For companies, incentives could include tax breaks or grants for developing and implementing retraining programs for their employees.

Regulatory Frameworks for AI Deployment: Develop regulatory frameworks that guide the ethical deployment of AI, ensuring that it complements human labour rather than simply replacing it. Regulations could encourage the use of AI for augmenting human capabilities and creating new job opportunities.

DEVELOPMENT OF A SOCIAL SAFETY NET

Universal Basic Income (UBI): Explore the feasibility of implementing a Universal Basic Income to provide financial security to all citizens, regardless of employment status. UBI could serve as a safety net for those affected by job displacement due to AI, allowing them to pursue retraining or education without financial hardship.

Healthcare and Social Services: Ensure access to healthcare and social services for displaced workers and those in transition between jobs. This includes mental health support, as job displacement and career transitions can be stressful experiences.

Portable Benefits: Develop portable benefits systems that are not tied to a specific employer, allowing workers to maintain their benefits as they move between jobs or engage in gig work. This flexibility is particularly important in an economy where freelance and contract work are becoming more common.

CONCLUSION

Navigating the employment impacts of AI requires proactive and comprehensive strategies that address the immediate challenges of job displacement and the longer-term need for workforce adaptation. By investing in education and retraining, implementing supportive policy interventions, and strengthening social safety nets, societies can ensure that the transition to an AI-driven economy is inclusive and beneficial for all workers. These efforts will be crucial in harnessing the potential of AI to generate economic growth and improve quality of life, while also mitigating its risks.

CHAPTER 9: THE FUTURE OF AI

ADVANCEMENTS IN AI TECHNOLOGY: WHAT'S NEXT?

The landscape of Artificial Intelligence (AI) is perpetually evolving, with machine learning algorithms at the heart of this transformation. As we look to the future, several key areas within machine learning are poised for significant advancements, potentially revolutionizing AI's learning capabilities and applications. This exploration delves into the evolution of deep learning, reinforcement learning, and the emergence of new paradigms in AI.

EVOLUTION OF DEEP LEARNING

Energy-Efficient Architectures: One of the next frontiers in deep learning involves developing more energy-efficient neural network architectures that can perform complex computations with less power. This advancement is crucial for scaling AI applications and making AI more sustainable and accessible.

Self-Supervised Learning: Moving beyond supervised learning, self-supervised learning represents a significant shift. By learning to predict parts of the input from other parts, AI systems can understand data in a more nuanced way, reducing the reliance on large labelled datasets and making AI more adaptable to diverse applications.

Neural Architecture Search (NAS): NAS uses machine learning to automate the design of neural network architectures. This approach can lead to the discovery of more efficient and effective models, tailored to specific tasks, and represents a leap towards more autonomous AI systems.

REINFORCEMENT LEARNING (RL) ADVANCEMENTS

Multi-Agent Systems: The development of multi-agent reinforcement learning, where multiple agents learn simultaneously in a shared environment, opens up possibilities for complex simulations, gaming, and real-world applications like traffic management and autonomous fleet coordination.

Transfer Learning in RL: Enhancing reinforcement learning models with transfer learning capabilities, where knowledge gained in one domain can be applied to others, is a key area of advancement. This approach can significantly speed up the learning process and broaden the applicability of RL models.

Safe Reinforcement Learning: As RL is increasingly applied in real-world scenarios, ensuring the safety of these systems becomes paramount. Research into safe reinforcement learning focuses on developing algorithms that can learn and operate within predefined safety constraints, minimizing risks to humans and the environment.

EMERGENCE OF NEW PARADIGMS

Federated Learning: This paradigm shifts the training of machine learning models to the edge, where data is generated. By training models across multiple decentralized devices while keeping the data localized, federated learning addresses privacy concerns and reduces the need for data centralization.

Quantum Machine Learning: Quantum computing promises to revolutionize machine learning by processing information in fundamentally new ways. Quantum machine learning could solve complex problems much faster than classical computers, from optimizing large systems to discovering new materials and drugs.

Neurosymbolic AI: Combining neural networks with symbolic reasoning, neurosymbolic AI aims to create systems that can not only process vast amounts of data but also understand and reason with abstract concepts. This hybrid approach could lead to AI systems with deeper understanding and reasoning capabilities, bridging the gap between human and machine intelligence.

CONCLUSION

The future of AI technology is marked by significant advancements in machine learning algorithms. From the evolution of deep learning and reinforcement learning to the emergence of new paradigms like federated learning and quantum machine learning, these developments promise to enhance AI's learning capabilities and expand its applications. As we venture into this future, the potential for AI to solve complex problems and transform industries continues to grow, heralding a new era of innovation and discovery.

POTENTIAL BREAKTHROUGHS IN AI HARDWARE

The relentless pursuit of advancements in Artificial Intelligence (AI) is not only a software-centric endeavour but also increasingly focuses on innovations in hardware technologies. Two of the most promising areas in AI hardware that have the potential to overcome current limitations in processing power and energy efficiency are quantum computing and neuromorphic chips. These technologies represent a paradigm shift in how data is processed and analysed, offering breakthrough capabilities that could significantly accelerate AI's evolution.

QUANTUM COMPUTING

Quantum computing harnesses the principles of quantum mechanics to process information in fundamentally new ways. Unlike classical computers, which use bits as the smallest unit of data (either a 0 or a 1), quantum computers use quantum bits or qubits, which can represent and store information in both 0 and 1 simultaneously thanks to superposition. Additionally, through a phenomenon known as entanglement, qubits can be correlated with each other, meaning the state of one (whether it's a 0, a 1, or both) can depend on the state of another, even across vast distances.

Overcoming Processing Power Limitations: Quantum computers have the potential to perform complex calculations exponentially faster than the best supercomputers today. This capability could revolutionize fields that require processing vast datasets or performing intricate simulations, such as drug discovery, climate modelling, and, notably, machine learning algorithms, by dramatically reducing computation times.

Energy Efficiency: Quantum computing could also address the growing concern over the energy consumption of traditional computing infrastructures. By performing calculations more efficiently and at speeds unattainable by classical computers, quantum computers could reduce the energy required for data-intensive AI tasks.

NEUROMORPHIC CHIPS

Neuromorphic computing seeks to mimic the human brain's architecture and operation, offering an alternative approach to traditional computing paradigms. Neuromorphic chips are designed to simulate the brain's neural networks, utilizing a vast array of interconnected neurons and synapses capable of parallel processing and dynamic learning.

Mimicking Brain Efficiency: The human brain is remarkably energy-efficient, capable of performing complex tasks like image recognition with a fraction of the power required by conventional computers. Neuromorphic chips aim to replicate this efficiency, potentially revolutionizing AI applications by enabling more powerful and energy-efficient processing.

Real-time Learning and Adaptation: Unlike traditional hardware, which relies on separate processing and memory units, neuromorphic chips can process and store information simultaneously, akin to how neurons process and remember information. This feature allows for real-time learning and adaptation without the need for extensive data transmission between the processor and memory, reducing latency and energy consumption.

CHALLENGES AND FUTURE DIRECTIONS

While quantum computing and neuromorphic chips hold immense promise, significant challenges remain. Quantum computing, for instance, requires extremely low temperatures to function, and maintaining quantum coherence over time is a complex issue. Similarly, neuromorphic computing is still in its infancy, with ongoing research needed to fully realize its potential and integrate it into mainstream AI applications.

CONCLUSION

The development of quantum computing and neuromorphic chips represents the cutting edge of AI hardware advancements. These technologies offer the potential to overcome current limitations in processing power and energy efficiency, paving the way for more powerful, efficient, and capable AI systems. As research and development continue, the next few decades could see these breakthroughs transforming the landscape of AI and computing, enabling new applications and capabilities that are currently beyond our reach.

ADVANCEMENTS IN (NLP) AND COMPUTER VISION

Advancements in Natural Language Processing (NLP) and Computer Vision represent two of the most dynamic and impactful areas within Artificial Intelligence (AI), significantly enhancing machines' ability to understand and interpret human language and visual information. These technologies are rapidly evolving, promising to bridge the gap between human capabilities and machine understanding further. Here's an examination of the advancements in these fields and their implications for the future.

ADVANCEMENTS IN NATURAL LANGUAGE PROCESSING (NLP)

NLP has seen remarkable progress in recent years, driven by the development of more sophisticated models and algorithms that enable a deeper understanding of language nuances, context, and semantics.
Contextual Understanding and Language Models: The advent of transformer-based models like BERT (Bidirectional Encoder Representations from Transformers) and GPT (Generative Pre-trained Transformer) has revolutionized NLP. These models can understand the context of words in sentences, capturing subtleties, idioms, and even humour, which were challenging for earlier models. Future advancements are expected to refine these capabilities, allowing for even more nuanced understanding and generation of human language.

Multilingual and Cross-lingual Models: NLP is becoming increasingly multilingual, with models being developed that can understand and translate between multiple languages, often without direct translation training data (zero-shot translation). This advancement will likely continue, breaking down language barriers and enabling more seamless cross-cultural communication.

Emotion and Sentiment Analysis: NLP technologies are improving in detecting and interpreting emotions and sentiments in text. This capability is crucial for applications ranging from customer service bots that can better respond to human emotions to mental health applications that monitor users' well-being through their language use.

ADVANCEMENTS IN COMPUTER VISION

Computer Vision has made significant strides in enabling machines to interpret and understand visual data from the world around them, from recognizing faces to understanding complex scenes.

Image and Video Recognition: Advances in deep learning have led to models that can accurately identify objects, people, and activities in images and videos with high precision. Future developments are expected to enhance these systems' accuracy and speed, enabling real-time processing of complex visual scenes on a large scale.

Generative Models: Generative Adversarial Networks (GANs) and Variational Autoencoders (VAEs) are at the forefront of creating realistic images and videos. These technologies have applications in entertainment, design, and even scientific research, where they can generate new data for analysis. Future advancements may lead to more realistic and customizable content generation, blurring the lines between generated and real visual content.

Augmented Reality (AR) and Virtual Reality (VR): Computer vision is a critical component of AR and VR technologies, enabling these systems to interact intelligently with real-world environments. Future advancements in computer vision will likely lead to more immersive and interactive AR/VR experiences, with applications in education, training, gaming, and remote work.

CONCLUSION

The future advancements in NLP and Computer Vision are set to further diminish the boundaries between human and machine capabilities in understanding language and visual information. These technologies will become more sophisticated in interpreting the world around us, leading to innovative applications that can enhance communication, understanding, and interaction with our environment. As these fields continue to evolve, they promise to unlock new possibilities in how we live, work, and connect with each other and the digital world.

AI AND SOCIETY

SHAPING THE FUTURE TOGETHER

The integration of Artificial Intelligence (AI) into various facets of daily life is set to have profound societal impacts over the next decade. As AI technologies advance, they will significantly influence employment, education, and social interactions, presenting both opportunities and challenges. Understanding these potential impacts is crucial for ensuring that society can adapt effectively and harness the benefits of AI while mitigating its risks.

CHANGES IN EMPLOYMENT

Job Creation and Displacement: AI is expected to automate many tasks currently performed by humans, leading to job displacement in certain sectors such as manufacturing, transportation, and administrative roles. However, it will also create new jobs in AI development, data analysis, cybersecurity, and other tech-driven fields. Society will need to adapt by investing in retraining programs and education to prepare the workforce for these new opportunities.

Shift Towards Gig Economy: AI and automation may accelerate the shift towards a gig economy, where short-term contracts or freelance work are prevalent. This shift could lead to more flexible work arrangements but also raise concerns about job security and benefits. Adapting to this change will require rethinking labour laws and social safety nets to protect gig economy workers.

CHANGES IN EDUCATION

Personalized Learning: AI has the potential to revolutionize education through personalized learning platforms that adapt to each student's pace and learning style. This could lead to improved educational outcomes and greater accessibility. However, ensuring equitable access to these AI-driven educational tools will be crucial to prevent widening the educational gap.

Lifelong Learning: As the demand for new skills accelerates, lifelong learning will become increasingly important. AI can support this by providing accessible learning platforms for continuous education and skill development. Educational institutions and policymakers will need to promote a culture of lifelong learning and provide the necessary resources and infrastructure.

Enhanced Connectivity: AI-driven technologies, such as social media algorithms and virtual reality, can enhance connectivity and offer new ways for people to interact and form communities. However, there's also a risk of increased isolation and the creation of echo chambers that reinforce existing biases.

Ethical and Privacy Concerns: The use of AI in social interactions raises ethical and privacy concerns, including data collection practices and the potential for surveillance. Society will need to establish robust ethical guidelines and privacy protections to address these issues.

ADAPTING TO CHANGES

Policy and Regulatory Frameworks: Developing comprehensive policy and regulatory frameworks that address the employment, educational, and social implications of AI will be essential. These frameworks should promote innovation while protecting individuals' rights and well-being.

Public Awareness and Engagement: Increasing public awareness and engagement regarding AI's potential impacts and ethical considerations is crucial. This includes fostering public discussions, involving diverse stakeholders in decision-making processes, and promoting digital literacy.

Collaboration Across Sectors: Collaboration between governments, industry, academia, and civil society will be key to navigating the societal impacts of AI. This collaboration can drive the development of inclusive and equitable AI technologies that benefit all members of society.

CONCLUSION

The societal impacts of AI in the next decade will be far-reaching, affecting employment, education, and social interactions. While these changes present significant challenges, they also offer opportunities for growth and improvement. By proactively adapting to these changes through thoughtful policy, education, and collaboration, society can ensure that the future of AI is shaped in a way that maximizes its benefits and minimizes its risks, leading to a more inclusive and equitable future for all.

ETHICAL CONSIDERATIONS OF ADVANCED AI TECHNOLOGIES

The rapid advancement of Artificial Intelligence (AI) technologies brings to the forefront a range of ethical considerations that are critical to address. As AI systems increasingly participate in or even autonomously carry out decision-making processes, the implications for individuals and society as a whole are profound. Ensuring that AI systems align with human values and ethics is paramount to harnessing their potential responsibly. This discussion explores the ethical considerations surrounding advanced AI technologies, focusing on their role in decision-making and the importance of alignment with human values.

ETHICAL CONSIDERATIONS IN AI DECISION-MAKING

Transparency and Explain ability: One of the primary ethical concerns is the often opaque nature of AI decision-making, particularly with complex algorithms like deep learning. Decisions made by AI systems can significantly impact people's lives, especially in areas like healthcare, criminal justice, and employment. Therefore, it's crucial that these AI systems operate transparently and their decisions can be explained and understood by humans. This transparency ensures accountability and allows for the evaluation of decisions against ethical standards.

Bias and Fairness: AI systems are only as unbiased as the data they are trained on. Historical data can contain implicit biases, leading AI to perpetuate or even exacerbate these biases in its decision-making. Ethical AI development must involve identifying and mitigating biases within datasets and algorithms to ensure fairness, particularly in decisions that affect people's opportunities, well-being, and rights.

Privacy: AI's ability to analyze vast amounts of personal data raises significant privacy concerns. Ethical AI use must respect individuals' privacy rights, ensuring that data is used responsibly, with consent, and in ways that do not infringe on personal privacy. This is particularly important in surveillance applications and personalized services, where the line between beneficial personalization and invasive monitoring can be thin.

ENSURING AI ALIGNS WITH HUMAN VALUES AND ETHICS

Incorporating Ethical Principles in AI Development: Developing AI in accordance with explicitly defined ethical principles is essential. This involves integrating ethical considerations at every stage of the AI development process, from design to deployment. Principles such as beneficence (promoting well-being), non-maleficence (doing no harm), autonomy (respecting human agency), and justice (ensuring fairness) can guide ethical AI development.

Multi-stakeholder Engagement: Ethical AI development requires the involvement of diverse stakeholders, including ethicists, sociologists, legal experts, affected communities, and the general public. This engagement ensures that multiple perspectives are considered, and AI systems are developed and deployed in ways that reflect a broad range of human values and societal norms.

Regulatory and Governance Frameworks: Establishing robust regulatory and governance frameworks is critical to ensuring AI aligns with human values and ethics. These frameworks can set standards for ethical AI development, provide mechanisms for accountability and redress, and ensure that AI applications serve the public interest. International cooperation is also vital, as AI's impact crosses national boundaries.

CONCLUSION

The ethical considerations of advanced AI technologies, especially regarding decision-making processes, underscore the need for a principled approach to AI development and deployment. Ensuring AI systems align with human values and ethics is not just a technical challenge but a societal imperative. By addressing these ethical considerations proactively, through transparency, fairness, privacy protection, and multi-stakeholder engagement, we can guide AI development in a direction that respects human dignity, promotes societal well-being, and upholds justice and human rights.

THE ROLE OF AI IN ADDRESSING GLOBAL CHALLENGES

Artificial Intelligence (AI) holds transformative potential not just for business and industry, but also for addressing some of the most pressing global challenges. From climate change and healthcare to bridging the gap of inequality, AI technologies offer innovative solutions that could significantly contribute to sustainable development and social good. This exploration delves into how AI can be leveraged across these critical areas to foster positive change and drive progress towards a more equitable and sustainable future.

AI IN COMBATING CLIMATE CHANGE

Climate Modelling and Prediction: AI can enhance the accuracy of climate models, enabling more precise predictions about weather patterns, temperature changes, and extreme weather events. These insights are crucial for developing effective strategies to mitigate climate change impacts and for planning adaptation measures in vulnerable regions.

Energy Efficiency: AI technologies can optimize energy consumption in various sectors, from manufacturing to residential buildings, reducing greenhouse gas emissions. Smart grids, powered by AI, can also facilitate the integration of renewable energy sources into the power grid, enhancing the sustainability of energy systems.

Conservation Efforts: AI aids in biodiversity conservation by analysing data from satellite images and sensors to monitor wildlife populations, deforestation rates, and the health of ecosystems. This information is vital for conservation planning and for tracking the effectiveness of environmental protection measures.

AI IN HEALTHCARE

Disease Diagnosis and Treatment: AI algorithms can analyze medical images, genetic information, and patient data to assist in diagnosing diseases early and accurately. Moreover, AI can personalize treatment plans based on the patient's unique health profile, improving treatment outcomes and advancing precision medicine.

Epidemic Prediction and Response: AI models can predict the outbreak and spread of infectious diseases by analysing data from various sources, including social media, travel patterns, and health reports. These predictions enable timely responses to contain outbreaks and prevent pandemics.

Access to Healthcare: AI-powered telemedicine and mobile health applications can extend healthcare services to remote and underserved areas, reducing barriers to access and addressing healthcare disparities.

AI IN REDUCING INEQUALITY

Education: AI can democratize access to education through personalized learning platforms that adapt to each student's needs and pace, helping to overcome educational barriers. AI can also provide language translation services, making educational content accessible to non-native speakers.

Economic Inclusion: AI technologies can facilitate financial inclusion by enabling alternative credit scoring models that consider non-traditional data, allowing individuals without formal credit histories to access financial services.

Additionally, AI-driven platforms can connect small farmers and entrepreneurs in developing countries with markets, information, and resources, boosting their economic prospects.

Social Welfare Programs: Governments can use AI to enhance the efficiency and effectiveness of social welfare programs. By analysing data on social and economic indicators, AI can help identify communities in need, optimize the allocation of resources, and monitor the impact of social interventions.

CHALLENGES AND ETHICAL CONSIDERATIONS

While AI offers promising solutions to global challenges, its deployment must be guided by ethical considerations and a commitment to social good. This includes ensuring the responsible use of data, addressing biases in AI algorithms, and involving diverse stakeholders in the development and implementation of AI solutions. Moreover, there is a need for international collaboration to maximize AI's benefits across borders and to prevent widening the digital divide.

CONCLUSION

AI's role in addressing global challenges underscores its potential as a force for good in advancing sustainable development and social good. By leveraging AI in climate change mitigation, healthcare, and reducing inequality, we can make significant strides towards a more equitable and sustainable future. However, realizing this potential requires a concerted effort to navigate the ethical and societal implications of AI, ensuring that its benefits are widely shared and that it serves the interests of humanity as a whole.

THE ROLE OF REGULATION AND GOVERNANCE IN AI DEVELOPMENT

As Artificial Intelligence (AI) continues to evolve and permeate various aspects of daily life, the need for comprehensive regulation and governance becomes increasingly apparent. The objective is to harness AI's potential while mitigating risks and ensuring ethical development and deployment. This section investigates emerging trends in AI regulation and governance, focusing on international efforts to establish standards and guidelines for ethical AI.

GLOBAL REGULATORY EFFORTS

European Union's AI Regulation: The European Union (EU) has been at the forefront of establishing regulatory frameworks for AI. The proposed AI Act is a pioneering effort to create a comprehensive legal framework for AI, categorizing AI systems according to their risk levels and setting strict requirements for high-risk applications. This regulation emphasizes transparency, accountability, and the protection of fundamental rights.

OECD Principles on AI: The Organisation for Economic Co-operation and Development (OECD) has developed principles on AI, endorsed by over 40 countries. These principles advocate for AI that is innovative and trustworthy and that respects human rights and democratic values. The OECD also emphasizes the importance of international cooperation to ensure consistent standards.

G7 AI Guidelines: The G7 countries have agreed on AI guidelines that focus on human-centric AI development, promoting the ethical use of AI and ensuring it benefits society as a whole. These guidelines encourage transparency, explain ability, and fairness in AI systems.

NATIONAL STRATEGIES AND LEGISLATION

United States: The US has taken a sector-specific approach to AI regulation, with guidelines and principles issued by various federal agencies. The National AI Initiative Act aims to coordinate AI research and policy across the federal government, emphasizing the importance of leadership in AI innovation and ethical standards.

China: China's New Generation Artificial Intelligence Development Plan outlines the country's ambition to become a global leader in AI by 2030. It includes measures for governance and ethical standards, focusing on promoting AI while ensuring security and controllability.

United Kingdom: The UK has proposed an AI regulation approach that is pro-innovation but emphasizes safety and ethics. The UK's AI Council has produced an AI Roadmap, recommending a national AI strategy that includes governance frameworks to support ethical AI development.

ETHICAL FRAMEWORKS AND STANDARDS

IEEE Global Initiative on Ethics of Autonomous and Intelligent Systems: The IEEE has developed ethically aligned design principles for autonomous and intelligent systems, offering detailed guidelines to ensure that AI technologies prioritize human well-being in their design and use.

Partnership on AI: Founded by major tech companies, the Partnership on AI fosters collaboration between industry, civil society, and academia to develop best practices on AI ethics, fairness, and inclusivity.

CHALLENGES IN AI REGULATION AND GOVERNANCE

Balancing Innovation and Regulation: One of the main challenges in AI regulation is ensuring that governance structures protect society from potential harms without stifling innovation. Finding this balance requires ongoing dialogue between policymakers, technologists, and other stakeholders.

International Cooperation: Given AI's global impact, international cooperation is crucial for harmonizing regulatory approaches. This ensures that AI benefits are maximized across borders while addressing global challenges such as privacy, security, and ethical standards.

CONCLUSION

The emerging trends in AI regulation and governance reflect a growing consensus on the need for ethical frameworks, transparency, and accountability in AI development and deployment. International efforts to establish standards and guidelines are crucial for fostering a global AI ecosystem that is both innovative and aligned with human values. As AI technologies advance, continuous evaluation and adaptation of regulatory frameworks will be essential to address new challenges and ensure that AI contributes positively to society.

CHALLENGES AND OPPORTUNITIES IN CREATING A REGULATORY FRAMEWORK

Creating a regulatory framework for Artificial Intelligence (AI) that effectively balances the imperative of fostering innovation with the necessity of protecting society from potential risks presents a complex array of challenges and opportunities. The rapid pace of AI development, coupled with its broad applications across various sectors, necessitates a nuanced approach to regulation. This discussion explores the key challenges and opportunities inherent in crafting such a regulatory framework.

CHALLENGES IN AI REGULATION

Rapid Technological Advancement
The swift evolution of AI technologies often outpaces the ability of regulatory frameworks to adapt, leading to a lag in governance that can leave gaps in oversight. Ensuring regulations remain relevant and effective in the face of continuous innovation is a significant challenge.

Balancing Innovation and Regulation
Striking the right balance between encouraging technological innovation and implementing necessary safeguards is crucial. Overregulation could stifle creativity and slow the pace of AI advancements, while under regulation could expose society to unchecked risks, including privacy violations, security threats, and ethical concerns.

Global Consistency vs. Local Relevance
AI's global impact necessitates international cooperation in regulatory efforts. However, achieving consensus among nations with differing priorities, values, and levels of technological advancement is challenging. Moreover, regulations must be flexible enough to address local concerns and contexts while striving for global consistency.

Ethical and Societal Implications
AI technologies raise profound ethical and societal questions, from the potential for bias and discrimination to concerns about autonomy and job displacement. Developing regulations that address these complex issues, ensuring AI aligns with societal values and ethical principles, is a formidable challenge.

FOSTERING TRUST AND CONFIDENCE

Well-crafted regulations can increase public trust in AI technologies by ensuring they are safe, reliable, and ethical. This trust is essential for widespread adoption and acceptance of AI, paving the way for its benefits to be fully realized across society.

Encouraging Responsible Innovation
Regulatory frameworks can incentivize companies to prioritize ethical considerations and safety in the development of AI technologies. By setting clear guidelines and standards, regulations can guide responsible innovation, ensuring that advancements in AI contribute positively to society.

Protecting Rights and Promoting Equity
Regulations offer an opportunity to safeguard individual rights and promote equity in the age of AI. By addressing issues such as data privacy, bias, and access, regulatory frameworks can ensure that AI technologies are developed and deployed in ways that protect citizens and promote fairness.

Driving International Collaboration
The global nature of AI challenges encourages international collaboration in regulatory efforts. This collaboration can lead to the sharing of best practices, the development of common standards, and coordinated responses to transnational risks, strengthening the governance of AI worldwide.

CRAFTING THE FRAMEWORK

Developing a regulatory framework for AI that balances innovation with societal protection requires a multifaceted approach:

Adaptive and Flexible Regulation: Regulations should be designed to adapt to technological advancements, possibly through mechanisms like regulatory sandboxes that allow for experimentation under regulatory oversight.

Stakeholder Engagement: Involving a broad range of stakeholders, including technologists, ethicists, policymakers, and the public, in the regulatory process ensures diverse perspectives are considered, making regulations more robust and inclusive.

Focus on Outcomes: Rather than prescribing specific technological solutions, regulations should focus on desired outcomes, such as safety, privacy, and fairness. This approach allows for flexibility in how AI developers achieve these goals, encouraging innovation while ensuring societal protections.

CONCLUSION

The journey to create a regulatory framework for AI that harmonizes the need for innovation with societal protection is fraught with challenges but also ripe with opportunities. By fostering trust, encouraging responsible innovation, protecting rights, and promoting international collaboration, such a framework can guide the development and deployment of AI technologies in ways that maximize their benefits for society while mitigating potential risks.

THE ROLE OF PUBLIC AND PRIVATE PARTNERSHIPS IN AI GOVERNANCE

The governance of Artificial Intelligence (AI) is a multifaceted challenge that requires the collective effort of various sectors of society. Public and private partnerships (PPPs) play a crucial role in this context, offering a collaborative framework through which governments, industry, academia, and civil society can work together to shape the future of AI. Such partnerships are essential for ensuring that AI development and deployment are guided by a balanced perspective that considers ethical, societal, and economic implications. This examination delves into how these collaborations can benefit all stakeholders involved in AI governance.

FACILITATING ETHICAL AI DEVELOPMENT

Ethical Frameworks and Standards: Collaborations between public entities and private companies can lead to the development of shared ethical frameworks and standards for AI. Academia contributes by providing research-based insights into ethical considerations, while civil society organizations ensure that the public's voice and concerns are represented. This collective effort can result in comprehensive guidelines that encourage responsible AI development.

Best Practices for AI Use: PPPs can establish best practices for AI use that prioritize transparency, accountability, and fairness. Governments can enforce these practices through regulation, while industry players can implement them in AI development and deployment processes. Academia and civil society can monitor compliance and suggest improvements, ensuring these practices evolve with technological advancements.

PROMOTING INNOVATION AND ECONOMIC GROWTH

Fostering Innovation Ecosystems: By working together, the public and private sectors can create innovation ecosystems that support the growth of AI technologies. Governments can provide funding and policy support, while private companies bring in investment, expertise, and real-world applications. Academia contributes through research and development, and civil society can identify areas where AI can have a positive social impact.

Accelerating AI Adoption: PPPs can accelerate the adoption of AI across various sectors by pooling resources, knowledge, and networks. Governments can incentivize AI adoption through subsidies and tax breaks, while private companies can offer AI solutions tailored to specific industry needs. Academia can support this process by training skilled AI professionals, and civil society can help identify societal needs that AI can address.

ENSURING INCLUSIVE AND EQUITABLE AI BENEFITS

Bridging the Digital Divide: Collaborative efforts can focus on bridging the digital divide by ensuring equitable access to AI technologies. This includes initiatives to bring AI education and resources to underserved communities, supported by government policies, industry technologies, academic knowledge, and civil society advocacy.

Addressing AI's Societal Impacts: PPPs are well-positioned to address the broader societal impacts of AI, such as job displacement and privacy concerns. By working together, stakeholders can develop strategies for workforce retraining, create privacy protection measures, and ensure that the benefits of AI are distributed equitably across society.

ENHANCING GLOBAL COOPERATION

International Standards and Regulations: The global nature of AI technology necessitates international cooperation in its governance. PPPs can play a role in developing and advocating for international standards and regulations that ensure AI's ethical and equitable use worldwide. This includes collaboration not just within countries but also between them, fostering a global approach to AI governance.

Public and private partnerships in AI governance offer a dynamic and flexible approach to navigating the complex landscape of AI development and deployment. By leveraging the strengths and perspectives of governments, industry, academia, and civil society, these collaborations can promote ethical AI development, foster innovation and economic growth, ensure inclusive and equitable benefits, and enhance global cooperation. The success of AI governance will depend on the ability of these diverse stakeholders to work together towards shared goals, shaping the future of AI in a way that benefits all of humanity.

CHAPTER 10: GETTING STARTED WITH AI

LEARNING RESOURCES AND COMMUNITIES FOR AI ENTHUSIASTS

KEY ONLINE PLATFORMS FOR AI EDUCATION

The journey into Artificial Intelligence (AI), machine learning, and data science is facilitated significantly by the wealth of online educational resources available today. These platforms offer courses that cater to a wide range of learners, from beginners to those seeking advanced knowledge. Here's an exploration of key online platforms that are instrumental in AI education:

Coursera: Coursera partners with leading universities and companies to offer a wide array of AI, machine learning, and data science courses. Notable courses include Andrew Ng's "Machine Learning" and the "Deep Learning Specialization," which provide foundational knowledge and dive into more complex topics. Coursera's model allows learners to audit courses for free or opt for a paid version that includes certification.

edX: Similar to Coursera, edX offers courses from universities around the world, covering a broad spectrum of AI topics. Courses range from introductory to advanced levels, including the "MicroMasters" program in AI and "Data Science" by UC San Diego, which are designed to provide a comprehensive learning path for students.

Udacity: Udacity's "Nanodegree" programs are project-based and focus on practical skills in AI, machine learning, and related fields. These programs, such as the "Machine Learning Engineer Nanodegree" and the "AI for Healthcare Nanodegree," are developed in collaboration with industry leaders, ensuring the curriculum is aligned with current industry needs.

Specialized AI Learning Platforms: Beyond these broad platforms, there are specialized resources dedicated exclusively to AI and machine learning. For instance, fast.ai offers a practical deep learning course for coders, emphasizing the use of modern best practices. DeepLearning.AI also provides cutting-edge courses on deep learning, tailored to those looking to delve deeper into specific aspects of AI.

Kaggle: While primarily known as a platform for data science competitions, Kaggle also offers "Micro-Courses" that cover essential topics like Python, machine learning, and deep learning. The interactive platform allows learners to apply concepts immediately through Kaggle's in-browser coding environment.

MIT OpenCourseWare (OCW) and Stanford Online: For those looking for materials from academic institutions, MIT OCW and Stanford Online offer free access to course content, including lectures and assignments, from their AI and machine learning courses. This is ideal for learners who prefer self-directed study or want to supplement their knowledge with academic rigor.

ENGAGING WITH THE COMMUNITY

While online courses provide the foundational knowledge and skills in AI, engaging with the community is equally important. Platforms like GitHub offer a wealth of open-source projects where learners can contribute and learn from real-world applications. Stack Overflow and Reddit's r/MachineLearning are vibrant communities for asking questions, sharing knowledge, and staying updated on the latest in AI research and development.

CONCLUSION

The landscape of online education for AI is rich and varied, offering opportunities for learners at all levels to dive into this exciting field. By leveraging these platforms and engaging with the broader AI community, enthusiasts can build a solid foundation in AI principles, stay abreast of the latest advancements, and apply their knowledge to real-world problems.

Leverage Open Educational Resources: Discuss the importance of open educational resources, including open-source textbooks, freely available research papers, and pre-recorded lecture series from leading universities.

LEVERAGING OPEN EDUCATIONAL RESOURCES IN AI LEARNING

Open Educational Resources (OER) have emerged as a pivotal element in democratizing education, particularly in the rapidly evolving field of Artificial Intelligence (AI). These resources, encompassing open-source textbooks, freely available research papers, and pre-recorded lecture series from leading universities, play a crucial role in making AI education accessible to a broader audience. Here's an exploration of their importance:

OPEN-SOURCE TEXTBOOKS

Accessibility and Inclusivity: Open-source textbooks significantly lower the barriers to education by providing free access to high-quality educational materials. This is especially important in AI, where the pace of development means traditional textbooks can quickly become outdated. Open-source materials can be updated more frequently and easily by the community, ensuring learners have access to the most current information.

Collaboration and Improvement: Many open-source textbooks are collaborative efforts that allow educators, researchers, and practitioners to contribute, review, and update content. This collaborative approach ensures that the material is comprehensive, up-to-date, and includes a variety of perspectives, enhancing the learning experience.

FREELY AVAILABLE RESEARCH PAPERS

Staying Current with Advances: The field of AI is characterized by rapid innovation and development. Freely available research papers on platforms like arXiv and ResearchGate allow learners and professionals alike to stay abreast of the latest discoveries, methodologies, and debates within the community.

Fostering Innovation: Access to cutting-edge research encourages innovation by enabling learners to build upon existing work. This open access to knowledge facilitates the cross-pollination of ideas across different domains of AI, driving the field forward.

PRE-RECORDED LECTURE SERIES FROM LEADING UNIVERSITIES

High-Quality Education: Many leading universities, including MIT, Stanford, and Harvard, offer pre-recorded lecture series on AI topics. These lectures provide access to high-quality education from world-renowned experts, making elite educational resources available to anyone with an internet connection.

Flexibility in Learning: Pre-recorded lectures offer the flexibility to learn at one's own pace, accommodating different learning styles and schedules. This flexibility is particularly beneficial for working professionals and individuals in different time zones, enabling lifelong learning and continuous professional development.

THE ROLE OF OER IN AI EDUCATION

Promoting Equity in Education: OER play a vital role in promoting equity in education by ensuring that learners from diverse backgrounds have equal access to high-quality AI learning materials. This is crucial for fostering a diverse AI workforce that can address the ethical and societal implications of AI technologies from a broad range of perspectives.

Encouraging Practical Application: Many OER not only provide theoretical knowledge but also include datasets, code examples, and project ideas that encourage practical application. This hands-on approach is essential for developing the skills needed to succeed in the AI field.

CONCLUSION

Open Educational Resources are indispensable in the landscape of AI education, offering accessible, current, and high-quality materials that support both foundational learning and cutting-edge research. By leveraging OER, learners can navigate the complexities of AI, contribute to its development, and apply its principles to solve real-world problems. As the AI field continues to grow, the importance of OER in fostering an informed, innovative, and diverse community of AI practitioners cannot be overstated.

ENGAGING WITH AI COMMUNITIES AND FORUMS

In the rapidly evolving field of Artificial Intelligence (AI), communities and forums play a crucial role in fostering learning, collaboration, and innovation. Platforms like GitHub, Stack Overflow, Reddit's r/MachineLearning, and LinkedIn groups offer unique opportunities for AI enthusiasts to engage with peers, experts, and industry leaders. Here's how joining these communities can significantly enhance one's journey in AI.

GITHUB: A HUB FOR COLLABORATION AND LEARNING

Open-Source Projects: GitHub hosts a vast array of open-source AI projects, providing an invaluable resource for learners to explore real-world applications of AI. Engaging with these projects can offer practical experience and a deeper understanding of AI concepts.

Community Contributions: Contributing to open-source projects on GitHub can enhance learning through hands-on experience. It also offers the opportunity to receive feedback from the community, fostering improvement and skill development.

STACK OVERFLOW: A PLATFORM FOR PROBLEM-SOLVING

Q&A Support: Stack Overflow is renowned for its question-and-answer format, allowing users to seek help with specific AI programming issues. The platform's extensive archive of questions covers a wide range of AI topics, offering immediate assistance and learning opportunities.

Community Expertise: The Stack Overflow community includes experienced AI professionals and researchers. Engaging with this community can provide insights into best practices, coding standards, and innovative solutions to complex problems.

REDDIT'S R/MACHINELEARNING: A FORUM FOR DISCUSSION AND DISCOVERY

Latest Trends and Research: Reddit's r/MachineLearning forum is a vibrant community for discussing the latest trends, research findings, and developments in AI and machine learning. It's an excellent resource for staying updated on the field's cutting edge.

Community Engagement: Participating in discussions can offer new perspectives and insights, enhancing one's understanding of AI. The forum also provides opportunities to ask questions, share experiences, and receive guidance from fellow AI enthusiasts and experts.

LINKEDIN GROUPS: NETWORKING AND PROFESSIONAL GROWTH

Professional Networking: LinkedIn groups dedicated to AI and related fields offer a platform for professional networking. Engaging with these groups can connect individuals with potential mentors, collaborators, and employers in the AI industry.

Learning and Development: LinkedIn groups often share articles, webinars, and event information relevant to AI. These resources can aid in continuous learning and professional development, keeping members informed about industry trends and opportunities.

THE VALUE OF COMMUNITY ENGAGEMENT

Support and Mentorship: AI communities provide a supportive environment where members can seek advice, feedback, and mentorship. This support is invaluable for overcoming challenges and accelerating learning.

Collaboration Opportunities: Engaging with AI communities opens up opportunities for collaboration on projects, research, and even start-up ventures. Collaborative experiences can enrich one's portfolio and contribute to professional growth.

Diverse Perspectives: AI communities bring together individuals from diverse backgrounds and expertise levels. This diversity fosters a rich learning environment where members can gain a broad understanding of AI applications and ethical considerations.

CONCLUSION

Engaging with AI communities and forums is an essential aspect of navigating the AI landscape. These platforms offer support, mentorship, and unparalleled opportunities for collaboration and professional growth. By actively participating in these communities, AI enthusiasts can enhance their learning experience, stay abreast of the latest developments, and contribute to the broader AI ecosystem.

BUILDING YOUR FIRST AI PROJECT

A STEP-BY-STEP GUIDE

CHOOSING A PROBLEM TO SOLVE

Embarking on your first AI project is an exciting journey into solving real-world problems with technology. The first step, choosing a problem to solve, is crucial as it sets the direction for your project. Here's a guide to selecting a manageable and engaging problem for your inaugural AI endeavour.

IDENTIFY YOUR INTERESTS AND STRENGTHS

Follow Your Passion: Start by listing areas you're passionate about or problems you find intriguing. AI projects can span countless domains, from healthcare and environmental conservation to finance and education. Choosing a topic you're genuinely interested in will keep you motivated throughout the project.

Assess Your Skills: Consider your current skills and knowledge in AI, programming, and the domain of your interest. It's important to select a problem that matches your skill level or slightly stretches it. This balance ensures the project is challenging yet achievable.

LOOK FOR REAL-WORLD PROBLEMS

Solve Personal Pain Points: Reflect on challenges you or people around you face that could be addressed with AI. Solving a personal pain point not only provides a clear motivation but also gives you a direct insight into the problem.

Community and Social Issues: Explore community forums, social media, and news articles for issues that could benefit from AI solutions. Tackling a problem with social impact can be incredibly rewarding and may offer opportunities for collaboration and support.

DEFINE THE SCOPE

Narrow Down the Problem: A common pitfall is choosing a problem that's too broad. Narrow down the problem to a specific aspect that's manageable within your resources and timeframe. For instance, instead of aiming to "solve traffic congestion," focus on "optimizing traffic light sequences at a busy intersection."

Feasibility and Data Availability: Ensure the problem is feasible for an AI solution and that relevant data is accessible. Some AI projects require large datasets for training models. Check public data repositories or consider collecting your own data if the problem is unique.

SET CLEAR OBJECTIVES

Define Success: Establish what success looks like for your project. Setting clear, measurable objectives helps in planning your approach and evaluating the project's outcome. For example, if your project aims to predict stock prices, a success criterion could be achieving a certain accuracy level in predictions.

Iterative Approach: Be prepared to refine your problem statement as you progress. AI projects often involve an iterative process where initial results lead to new insights and adjustments in objectives.

SEEK FEEDBACK

Consult with Peers and Mentors: Before diving deep into your project, seek feedback on your chosen problem from peers, mentors, or members of AI communities. They can offer valuable perspectives on the problem's relevance, feasibility, and potential impact.

CONCLUSION

Choosing the right problem to solve is the foundation of a successful AI project. By aligning the problem with your interests, ensuring it's manageable, and setting clear objectives, you can embark on an AI project that's not only technically challenging but also personally rewarding and potentially impactful. Remember, the goal of your first AI project is as much about learning and growth as it is about solving the problem itself.

GATHER AND PREPARE YOUR DATA

After selecting a manageable and engaging problem for your AI project, the next crucial step is to gather and prepare your data. This phase is foundational, as the quality and appropriateness of your data directly influence the effectiveness of your AI model. Here's a comprehensive guide on how to navigate this critical stage.

Identify Data Sources: Based on the problem you've chosen, identify potential sources of data. These could include public data repositories like Kaggle, UCI Machine Learning Repository, or government databases. For more niche problems, consider using APIs from social media platforms, web scraping, or even creating datasets through surveys or experiments.

Assess Data Quality: Evaluate the quality of the data available. High-quality data should be relevant to your problem, accurately labelled (if applicable), and sufficiently comprehensive. Be cautious of datasets with many missing values or inconsistencies.

Ethical Considerations: When collecting data, especially personal or sensitive information, adhere to ethical guidelines and legal requirements. Ensure you have the right to use the data, respect privacy concerns, and obtain necessary permissions.

PREPARING THE DATA FOR ANALYSIS

Data Cleaning: Begin by cleaning your data, which involves removing or correcting inaccuracies, inconsistencies, and missing values in your dataset. This step might include deleting irrelevant entries, filling in missing values based on other data points, or entirely removing features that are not useful for your analysis.

Normalization and Feature Scaling: AI models often perform better when numerical input data is scaled or normalized. Techniques like Min-Max normalization or Z-score standardization ensure that all numerical features contribute equally to the model's training process.

Feature Engineering: Transform raw data into features that better represent the underlying problem to the predictive models. This process might involve creating new features from existing ones, encoding categorical variables, or reducing dimensionality to improve model performance and reduce computational complexity.

Splitting the Data: Divide your dataset into training, validation, and test sets. A common split ratio is 70% for training, 15% for validation, and 15% for testing. This separation is crucial for training your model, tuning hyperparameters, and finally evaluating the model's performance on unseen data.

Understand Your Data: Spend time exploring and understanding your data before jumping into model building. Use visualizations and statistics to get insights into the distribution, correlations, and potential biases in your data.

Iterative Process: Data preparation is rarely a linear process. Be prepared to iterate on this phase as you develop your model. Insights gained from initial model results can inform further data preparation steps.

Document Your Process: Keep detailed documentation of how you collect, clean, and prepare your data. This practice not only aids in reproducibility but also helps in troubleshooting and refining your model.

Seek Feedback: Especially if you're new to AI, getting feedback from more experienced practitioners on your data preparation process can be invaluable. Use forums, communities, or mentors to review your approach and suggest improvements.

CONCLUSION

Gathering and preparing your data is a meticulous but rewarding process that sets the foundation for your AI project. By ensuring your data is relevant, clean, and well-prepared, you significantly increase your project's chances of success. Remember, the goal of this phase is to transform raw data into a format that can effectively train your AI model, paving the way for meaningful insights and solutions to your chosen problem.

SELECT AND IMPLEMENT AN AI MODEL

After gathering and preparing your data, the next step in your AI project journey is to select and implement an appropriate AI model. This phase is crucial as the choice of model significantly impacts the performance and outcomes of your project. Here's a guide to navigating this process, considering the nature of your data and the complexity of the problem at hand.

CHOOSING AN APPROPRIATE AI MODEL

Understand the Problem Type: The first step in choosing an AI model is to clearly define the type of problem you are solving—whether it's classification, regression, clustering, or something else. Each problem type has models that are generally more suitable or performant.

Consider the Nature of Your Data: The characteristics of your dataset—such as size, quality, and feature types (categorical vs. numerical)—can influence the choice of model. For instance, deep learning models require large amounts of data, while decision trees or support vector machines might be more suitable for smaller datasets.

Evaluate Model Complexity: Consider the complexity of the model in relation to the complexity of your problem. While more complex models, like deep neural networks, can capture intricate patterns, they also require more data and computational resources. Sometimes, simpler models can achieve comparable performance with less complexity.

Review Literature and Benchmarks: Look for academic papers, articles, or open-source projects that have addressed similar problems. Insights from these sources can guide you towards models that have shown promising results in similar contexts.

IMPLEMENTING THE MODEL USING AI FRAMEWORKS

Select an AI Framework: Choose an AI framework or library that suits your needs and expertise level. Popular frameworks include TensorFlow, PyTorch, Scikit-learn, and Keras. These frameworks offer extensive documentation and community support, making them accessible to beginners and experts alike.

Prepare Your Development Environment: Set up your development environment by installing the necessary software, libraries, and dependencies. Many AI frameworks offer comprehensive guides to get you started.

Model Implementation: Begin by defining your model architecture. If you're using a deep learning framework, this involves specifying the layers, activation functions, and other parameters. For traditional machine learning models, frameworks like Scikit-learn provide pre-built estimators that simplify this process.

Deep Learning Models: Utilize frameworks like TensorFlow or PyTorch to build and train deep learning models. These frameworks allow for customization and are suited for complex problems requiring neural networks.

Traditional Machine Learning Models: For problems that might benefit from traditional machine learning approaches, use Scikit-learn or similar libraries that offer a wide range of algorithms with simpler implementation processes.

Training the Model: With your model defined, the next step is to train it using your prepared dataset. This involves feeding the training data into the model, adjusting the model's parameters based on its performance, and iterating until you achieve satisfactory results.

Validation and Testing: Use your validation set to tune hyperparameters and avoid overfitting. Once satisfied with the model's performance, evaluate it on the test set to assess its generalization to new, unseen data.

BEST PRACTICES

Experimentation: Be prepared to experiment with different models and configurations. AI model selection and implementation is often an iterative process, requiring adjustments based on performance and insights gained during training.

Documentation: Keep detailed records of the models tested, configurations used, and performance outcomes. This documentation is invaluable for refining your approach and communicating your findings.

Leverage Pre-trained Models: For deep learning projects, consider starting with pre-trained models, especially when data is limited. Fine-tuning a pre-trained model can significantly reduce development time and computational resources.

CONCLUSION

Selecting and implementing an AI model is a dynamic process that blends theoretical knowledge with practical experimentation. By carefully considering your problem type, data characteristics, and available resources, and by leveraging the power of AI frameworks, you can navigate this phase effectively. Remember, the goal is not just to build a model but to develop a solution that addresses your chosen problem in a meaningful way.

EVALUATE AND ITERATE

After selecting and implementing an AI model, the next crucial steps are to evaluate its performance and iterate on the design to improve results. This iterative process is essential for refining your AI project and ensuring it effectively addresses the problem at hand. Here's how to navigate the evaluation and iteration phases of your AI project.

EVALUATING THE PERFORMANCE OF THE AI MODEL

Choose the Right Metrics: The choice of evaluation metrics should align with the nature of your problem and the objectives of your project. For classification tasks, metrics like accuracy, precision, recall, and F1 score are commonly used. For regression tasks, mean absolute error (MAE) and root mean squared error (RMSE) are typical metrics. Selecting appropriate metrics is crucial for meaningful evaluation.

Use a Validation Set: Evaluate your model's performance on a validation set that was not used during training. This helps assess how well your model generalizes to new, unseen data. If your model performs well on the training set but poorly on the validation set, it may be overfitting.

Cross-Validation: For a more robust evaluation, consider using cross-validation techniques, especially if your dataset is limited. Cross-validation involves dividing your dataset into multiple subsets and training and evaluating your model multiple times, each time with a different subset held out for validation.

ITERATING ON THE DESIGN

Adjusting Parameters: Based on the initial evaluation, adjust your model's hyperparameters to improve performance. This might include learning rate, the number of layers in a neural network, or the depth of a decision tree. Hyperparameter tuning can be done manually, through grid search, or using automated methods like random search or Bayesian optimization.

Refining the Dataset: If your model is underperforming, revisit your dataset. Look for ways to enhance data quality through additional cleaning, feature engineering, or by addressing class imbalances. Sometimes, collecting more data or augmenting the existing dataset can significantly improve model performance.

Experiment with Different Models: If adjustments to parameters and data do not yield the desired improvements, consider experimenting with different AI models. Sometimes, a different algorithm or a more complex model architecture may be better suited to your problem.

BEST PRACTICES FOR ITERATION

Iterative Approach: Model development in AI is inherently iterative. Be prepared to cycle through the process of training, evaluating, and adjusting multiple times before achieving optimal results.

Document Iterations: Keep detailed records of each iteration, including the model configuration, evaluation metrics, and any changes made. This documentation is invaluable for tracking progress, understanding the impact of adjustments, and guiding future projects.

Seek Feedback: Engage with peers, mentors, or the AI community to get feedback on your approach and results. External insights can provide new perspectives and suggestions for improvement.

Be Patient: Achieving the best model performance can take time and requires patience. Each iteration provides learning opportunities and brings you closer to your project goals.

CONCLUSION

Evaluating and iterating on your AI model are critical steps in the development process. Through careful evaluation using appropriate metrics and a willingness to adjust parameters, refine the dataset, or even change models, you can enhance your project's effectiveness. Remember, the goal of iteration is not just to improve model performance but also to deepen your understanding of the problem and the data, contributing to your growth as an AI practitioner.

CAREERS IN AI: PATHS AND POSSIBILITIES

The field of Artificial Intelligence (AI) offers a wide array of career paths, reflecting its diverse applications across various industries. From technical roles focused on developing AI models to positions cantered around the ethical use of AI, the opportunities are vast and varied. Here's an overview of some key career paths within AI, along with insights into the industries where AI skills are in high demand.

KEY AI CAREER PATHS

Data Scientist: Data scientists analyze and interpret complex data to help companies make informed decisions. They use machine learning algorithms to predict outcomes and uncover patterns in data. This role requires a strong foundation in statistics, programming, and data analysis.

Machine Learning Engineer: Machine Learning Engineers are responsible for designing and implementing machine learning applications and systems. They work closely with data scientists to create algorithms based on predictive models and deploy these models to production environments.

AI Research Scientist: AI Research Scientists push the boundaries of what is possible in AI. They conduct high-level research on machine learning algorithms, neural networks, and other computational techniques. This role typically requires a Ph.D. or extensive experience in the field and involves publishing research findings, developing new AI technologies, and contributing to the scientific community.

AI Ethics Officer: As AI technologies become more integrated into society, the need for ethical guidelines and governance increases. AI Ethics Officers ensure that AI applications are developed and used responsibly, adhering to ethical standards and societal norms. They address issues related to privacy, bias, transparency, and the impact of AI on employment and society.

Robotics Engineer: Robotics Engineers design and build robots that can perform tasks autonomously or assist humans. AI plays a crucial role in robotics, enabling robots to process sensory information and make decisions. This field combines knowledge of AI, engineering, and computer science.

INDUSTRIES WHERE AI SKILLS ARE IN DEMAND

Technology: The tech industry is at the forefront of AI development, offering roles in software companies, start-ups, and large tech firms. AI applications in tech include natural language processing, computer vision, and recommendation systems.

Finance: AI is transforming the finance industry through algorithmic trading, fraud detection, customer service chatbots, and personalized financial advice. Professionals with AI skills can find opportunities in banks, investment firms, and fintech start-ups.

Healthcare: AI is revolutionizing healthcare by improving diagnostic accuracy, personalizing treatment plans, and optimizing patient care management. Careers in AI within healthcare include working on medical imaging analysis, drug discovery, and health informatics.

Entertainment: The entertainment industry uses AI for content recommendation, virtual reality experiences, and even in the creation of music and art. AI professionals can contribute to enhancing user experiences in gaming, streaming services, and digital media.

Automotive: With the advent of autonomous vehicles, the automotive industry offers exciting opportunities for AI professionals. Roles include developing algorithms for self-driving cars, enhancing vehicle safety systems, and optimizing traffic management.

CONCLUSION

Careers in AI are diverse, spanning technical, ethical, and research-oriented roles across multiple industries. As AI continues to evolve, the demand for skilled professionals in this field is expected to grow, offering exciting opportunities for innovation and impact. Whether you're interested in developing cutting-edge AI technologies, applying AI to solve industry-specific problems, or ensuring the responsible use of AI, there's a career path in AI suited to your interests and skills.

SKILLS AND QUALIFICATIONS FOR A CAREER IN AI

Pursuing a career in Artificial Intelligence (AI) requires a blend of technical skills, foundational knowledge, and soft skills. The interdisciplinary nature of AI means that professionals often need to draw on expertise from computer science, mathematics, domain-specific knowledge, and more. Here's a breakdown of the essential skills and qualifications for a successful career in AI.

TECHNICAL SKILLS

Programming Languages: Proficiency in programming languages is fundamental. Python is the most widely used language in AI due to its simplicity and the extensive libraries available, such as TensorFlow and PyTorch. Other important languages include R for statistical analysis, Java, and C++ for system-level programming.

Machine Learning and Deep Learning: Understanding machine learning algorithms—from linear regression to complex neural networks—is crucial. This includes knowledge of how to implement these algorithms, adjust parameters, and use frameworks and libraries to build models.

Statistics and Probability: AI heavily relies on statistical methods and probability to make predictions and understand data patterns. A strong grasp of statistics, including concepts like distributions, hypothesis testing, and Bayesian thinking, is essential.

Data Modelling and Evaluation: The ability to model data effectively and evaluate the performance of AI models is key. This includes understanding how to pre-process data, choose the right model, and use metrics to assess accuracy, precision, recall, and other performance indicators.

FOUNDATIONAL KNOWLEDGE

Algorithms and Data Structures: A solid understanding of algorithms and data structures is necessary for optimizing AI models and ensuring they run efficiently.

Mathematics: Linear algebra, calculus, and discrete mathematics form the mathematical backbone of AI. These areas are critical for understanding how algorithms work and for developing new AI models.

SOFT SKILLS

Critical Thinking and Problem-Solving: AI professionals must be able to approach complex problems systematically, analyze various solutions, and solve problems creatively. Critical thinking enables the evaluation of different AI approaches and the anticipation of potential challenges.

Communication: Effective communication skills are vital for collaborating with team members, explaining technical concepts to non-experts, and presenting findings. Being able to articulate the implications and limitations of AI models is particularly important.

Ethical Judgment: As AI technologies can have significant societal impacts, professionals need to possess ethical judgment to navigate issues related to privacy, bias, and fairness. Understanding the ethical considerations of deploying AI systems is increasingly becoming a requisite skill.

Adaptability and Continuous Learning: The field of AI is rapidly evolving, requiring professionals to be adaptable and committed to continuous learning. Staying abreast of the latest research, tools, and technologies is necessary for success.

QUALIFICATIONS

Educational Background: While many AI positions require a bachelor's degree in computer science, mathematics, or related fields, advanced roles may require a master's degree or Ph.D., especially for research-oriented positions.

Certifications and Specializations: Certifications from reputable organizations or completion of specialized courses in AI, machine learning, and data science can enhance a candidate's qualifications, especially for those transitioning from other fields.

CONCLUSION

A career in AI demands a mix of technical prowess, foundational knowledge, and soft skills. Aspiring AI professionals should focus on building a strong technical foundation while also developing the critical soft skills needed to navigate the complexities and ethical considerations of AI. Continuous learning and adaptability are key, as the field is characterized by rapid advancements and evolving challenges.

NAVIGATING THE AI JOB MARKET

Entering the AI job market can be a challenging yet rewarding endeavour. As the demand for AI expertise continues to grow across various industries, positioning yourself as a qualified candidate involves more than just acquiring the necessary technical skills. Here are strategies to effectively navigate the AI job market and enhance your employability.

Professional Networking Events and Conferences: Attend AI-related conferences, workshops, and meetups to connect with professionals in the field. These events are excellent opportunities to learn from experts, discover potential job openings, and make connections that could lead to job referrals.

Online Communities: Engage with online AI communities on platforms like LinkedIn, GitHub, Reddit (e.g., r/MachineLearning), and Stack Overflow. Participating in discussions, sharing your projects, and contributing to open-source projects can increase your visibility and establish your reputation in the AI community.

Alumni Networks: Leverage alumni networks from your educational institutions. Many universities have alumni groups focused on AI and technology, which can be valuable resources for networking and mentorship.

BUILDING A PORTFOLIO OF AI PROJECTS

Showcase Real-World Applications: Develop a portfolio of AI projects that demonstrate your skills and ability to apply AI techniques to solve real-world problems. Include a variety of projects that showcase different aspects of AI, such as machine learning models, data analysis, and natural language processing applications.

Use Public Datasets: Utilize public datasets to create projects if you don't have access to proprietary data. This can also demonstrate your ability to work with different types of data and extract meaningful insights.

Document Your Projects: For each project in your portfolio, include a detailed description of the problem, your approach, the technologies used, and the outcomes. Make your code available on GitHub and consider writing blog posts or creating videos to explain your projects further.

PURSUING INTERNSHIPS

Gain Practical Experience: Internships offer valuable hands-on experience and a glimpse into working on AI in a professional setting. They can also lead to full-time job offers or valuable connections in the industry.

Explore Various Industries: AI applications span numerous industries. Pursuing internships in different sectors can help you identify the areas you're most passionate about and where you'd like to focus your career.

STAYING ABREAST OF INDUSTRY TRENDS AND EMERGING TECHNOLOGIES

Continuous Learning: The AI field is rapidly evolving, with new technologies, tools, and methodologies emerging regularly. Stay informed by following AI research, attending webinars, and taking online courses to keep your skills up-to-date.

Industry Publications and Influencers: Follow industry publications, blogs, and influencers to stay informed about the latest trends and developments in AI. This can also provide insights into the skills and expertise currently in demand.

Specialization: Consider specializing in a niche area of AI where demand is growing, such as AI ethics, healthcare applications, or autonomous vehicles. Specialization can make you more attractive to employers looking for specific expertise.

CONCLUSION

Navigating the AI job market successfully requires a combination of solid technical skills, practical experience, and effective networking. By building a robust portfolio of projects, pursuing internships, and staying current with industry trends, you can enhance your visibility and attractiveness to potential employers. Remember, the journey into an AI career is a continuous learning process, where adaptability and a proactive approach to professional development are key to long-term success.

THE IMPORTANCE OF CONTINUOUS LEARNING IN AI

The field of Artificial Intelligence (AI) is characterized by rapid advancements and constant evolution. This dynamic nature necessitates a commitment to lifelong learning for professionals aiming to remain relevant and competitive. Continuous learning is not just a means to keep up with the latest developments; it's a fundamental aspect of thriving in the AI landscape. Here are key reasons why continuous learning is crucial in AI and practical ways to engage in ongoing professional development.

WHY CONTINUOUS LEARNING IS ESSENTIAL IN AI

Keeping Pace with Technological Advancements: AI technologies and methodologies are continually evolving, with new algorithms, tools, and best practices emerging regularly. Staying informed about these developments ensures that professionals can apply the most effective solutions to AI challenges.

Enhancing Career Prospects: Professionals who actively update their skills and knowledge are more likely to advance in their careers. Continuous learning demonstrates a commitment to excellence and adaptability, qualities highly valued in the AI field.

Fostering Innovation: Exposure to new ideas and technologies through continuous learning can inspire innovative approaches to problem-solving. This not only contributes to personal growth but also drives progress in the field of AI.

WAYS TO ENGAGE IN CONTINUOUS LEARNING

Attending Workshops and Conferences: Participating in AI workshops and conferences is an excellent way to learn about cutting-edge research, network with peers, and gain insights from leaders in the field. Many conferences now offer virtual attendance options, making them more accessible.

Online Courses and Specializations: Platforms like Coursera, edX, Udacity, and others offer courses and specializations in various AI domains. These courses range from introductory to advanced levels, allowing professionals to build new skills or deepen existing expertise.

Pursuing Advanced Degrees or Certifications: For those looking to make significant advancements in their AI knowledge, pursuing an advanced degree (such as a Master's or Ph.D.) in AI, machine learning, or data science can be a valuable investment. Alternatively, professional certifications in AI technologies and tools can validate skills and enhance one's resume.

Joining AI Communities and Forums: Engaging with AI communities, both online and offline, can provide continuous learning opportunities. Forums like Stack Overflow, Reddit's r/MachineLearning, and GitHub offer platforms to discuss AI trends, share projects, and seek advice.

Reading AI Research and Publications: Keeping up with AI research papers, blogs, and publications is crucial for staying informed about the latest developments. Websites like arXiv and Google Scholar, as well as AI-focused blogs and newsletters, are valuable resources.

Personal Projects and Experimentation: Working on personal AI projects or participating in competitions like those on Kaggle can challenge you to apply your skills in new ways and learn through doing. These projects can also be a great addition to your professional portfolio.

CONCLUSION

Continuous learning is the cornerstone of a successful career in AI. Given the field's rapid pace of change, professionals must actively seek opportunities to learn and grow. By embracing a mindset of lifelong learning and leveraging the myriad resources available, AI professionals can ensure they remain at the forefront of technological innovation and continue to contribute meaningfully to the advancement of the field.

FURTHER READING AND RESOURCES

BOOKS, WEBSITES, COURSES, AND COMMUNITIES

BOOKS

1. "Artificial Intelligence: A Guide for Thinking Humans" by Melanie Mitchell
An accessible overview of AI and its implications for society, thoughtfully critiquing the hype surrounding AI.

2. "Life 3.0: Being Human in the Age of Artificial Intelligence" by Max Tegmark
Explores the future of AI and its impact on the very fabric of human existence, presenting scenarios that range from utopian to dystopian.

3. "Superintelligence: Paths, Dangers, Strategies" by Nick Bostrom
A deep dive into the risks and ethics of AI, particularly focusing on the potential future of super intelligent systems.

4. "Deep Learning" by Ian Goodfellow, Yoshua Bengio, and Aaron Courville
For those seeking a technical understanding, this book offers comprehensive insights into deep learning techniques and theories.

WEBSITES

1. ArXiv (arxiv.org)
A free distribution service and an open-access archive for scholarly articles in the fields of physics, mathematics, computer science, quantitative biology, quantitative finance, and statistics, including AI and deep learning.

2. MIT Technology Review (technologyreview.com)
Provides insightful analysis and commentary on the latest in technology, including significant advancements in AI.

3. OpenAI (openai.com)
A research and deployment company that aims to ensure that artificial general intelligence benefits all of humanity. Their blog and research publications are great resources.

4. Google AI Blog (ai.googleblog.com)
Offers updates and insights from Google researchers and engineers on their latest AI developments.

COURSES

1. "AI For Everyone" by Andrew Ng on Coursera
A non-technical course that provides a broad introduction to AI, its capabilities, and its impact on society.

2. "Machine Learning" by Andrew Ng on Coursera
A foundational course that introduces the core idea of teaching a computer to learn concepts using data—without being explicitly programmed.

3. "Deep Learning Specialization" by Andrew Ng on Coursera
A series of comprehensive courses that dive deep into the nuts and bolts of deep learning, neural networks, and machine learning projects.

4. "Introduction to Artificial Intelligence (AI)" by Microsoft on edX
Offers a grounding in AI concepts and technologies, emphasizing their business and ethical implications.

Communities

1. Reddit: r/MachineLearning
A vibrant community for machine learning enthusiasts to discuss and share the latest in AI research and applications.

2. Stack Overflow
While not AI-specific, it's a crucial resource for troubleshooting coding and implementation issues in AI projects.

3. GitHub
A platform for hosting and reviewing code, managing projects, and building software alongside millions of other developers, including AI projects and collaborations.

4. Deep Learning AI Slack Channel
An invite-only community where AI practitioners gather to discuss deep learning research, projects, and ideas.

ACKNOWLEDGMENTS

This book represents not just my journey through the fascinating world of Artificial Intelligence (AI) but also the collective wisdom, efforts, and pioneering spirit of many who have contributed to this field. I am deeply grateful to a multitude of individuals and entities whose work has significantly influenced and enriched this manuscript.

First and foremost, my heartfelt thanks go to the academic and research community for their relentless pursuit of knowledge and innovation in AI. The works of esteemed researchers and educators, particularly those whose courses and lectures are freely available online, have been invaluable. Platforms like Coursera, edX, Udacity, and others deserve special mention for democratizing access to learning and for being treasure troves of knowledge.

I extend my gratitude to the vibrant online communities, including GitHub, Stack Overflow, and Reddit's r/MachineLearning, whose members have been generous with their knowledge, support, and feedback. These forums have not only provided insights and solutions to myriad challenges but also fostered a sense of camaraderie among AI enthusiasts and professionals.

Special thanks to the creators and maintainers of open-source tools and libraries that have been instrumental in the development of AI technologies. Your contributions have been crucial in advancing the field and empowering others to innovate and create.

I must acknowledge the role of public data repositories and the researchers who share their findings openly. Your commitment to open science and data sharing has significantly broadened the horizons of what is possible in AI research and application.

To my peers and mentors in the AI community, your guidance, encouragement, and critique have been pivotal in shaping this book. Your wisdom and experiences have not only informed the content herein but also inspired me to delve deeper into the complexities of AI.

My deepest appreciation goes to my family and friends for their unwavering support and patience throughout the process of writing this book. Your belief in my work and your constant encouragement have been my strength.

Lastly, I thank you, the reader, for embarking on this exploration of AI with me. It is my sincere hope that this book serves as both a guide and an inspiration for your own journey in AI, whether you are a student, a professional, or simply an AI enthusiast. Together, let us continue to push the boundaries of what AI can achieve for the betterment of society and the world at large.